Remnants

THE MAKER'S MARK
REMNANTS

Edited by Jon Garrad

freak ash
BOOKS

Published in the United Kingdom in 2007 by Freak Ash Books,
a trade name of Freak Ash Ltd.

First Edition

Acknowledgements:

Crowdance, by Gregory A. T. Morris
My Brother's Keeper, by Robin Kate Harding
The Price Of Gold, by Lawrence Duncalf
Legacy Of Life, by Nick Westwood
Cayuse, by Colleen Weare
Perfection, by Will Isgrove and Jon Garrad
Every Sheep Needs A Shepherd, by Jeffery Pagenton
Top Night Out, by Jon Garrad
Escape From Migration, by Anthony Burn
Inheritance, by Erin Hockings

reproduced with permission from the authors. The right of these
individuals to be identified as the authors of their respective
works has been asserted by them in accordance with the
Copyright, Designs and Patents Act, 1988

Edited by Jon Garrad
Artwork by Huw Davies
Design and layout by Simon Burn

A catalogue record for this book is available from the
British library

ISBN 978 0 9553403 5 2

Printed and bound by Trade Print Europe Ltd, London
72 New Bond Street, London, W1S 1RR

Contents

CROWDANCE   1
Gregory A. T. Morris

MY BROTHER'S KEEPER   19
Robin Kate Harding

THE PRICE OF GOLD   33
Lawrence Duncalf

LEGACY OF LIFE   57
Nick Westwood

CAYUSE   87
Colleen Weare

PERFECTION   105
Will Isgrove and Jon Garrad

EVERY SHEEP NEEDS A SHEPHERD   121
Jeffery Pagenton

TOP NIGHT OUT   143
Jon Garrad

ESCAPE FROM MIGRATION   165
Anthony Burn

INHERITANCE   187
Erin Hockings

AFTERWORD   201

Crowdance

GREGORY A. T. MORRIS

WIND WHISTLED THROUGH THE STREETS OF CROWDANCE, BRUSHING up dust and throwing it a few feet onwards to find a new home somewhere else. It was always dead quiet in town after the miners left, especially compared to the noise they brought with them. Every two weeks the mines on Big Thorn Mountain emptied out and all the miners came back into town whooping and hollering and kicking up a fuss. They spent so much time buried, plucking chunks of ore from near-inexhaustible seams, that when they got above ground they became different men. The town filled with movement and colour and men trying to pack as much action into as little time as possible to relieve the stress of their regular life. Sitting in the darkness hammering at rock with a bit of metal on a stick could do things to a droid, and seemed to do so with alarming frequency.

Most of them never really talked about it. They just made a ruckus: fighting, brawling, boasting, and blowing holes in buildings which happened to be at the wrong spot when a real fight broke out. There was Miss Lucy, boarding over another hole in the side of her boarding house. She never complained much, as the miners paid her rates and didn't ask for anything too fancy. Some of the miners tried to give her something extra to help her along when they came into town, but she was too proud to accept it. Little Jimmy nodded to her as he caught her eye in passing. She smiled, a little flustered from the effort of balancing on the stepladder and hammering in nails under the hot sun.

Sadler's General Store was closing for lunch, Skinny Sadler turning the sign in the front window around and drawing the blinds halfway. He was getting crotchety in his old age, not that he'd ever been particularly agreeable to anyone who wasn't spending money in his store anyway. But now he flat-out refused to stay open while he was having his lunch, and he was opening later and closing earlier as well. His was the only store in town, though, and there was no reason for anyone else to open competition. For one thing there'd be no place to put it. Main Street — the only street in town, really — was full up. Not that it was too hard to do: Crowdance wasn't all that big anyway. The rows of houses and stores had just kind of grown up around the assayer's office, the post office, and Sadler's store.

Mining was why Crowdance existed. The need for ore brought men to the mountains and the constant demand kept them there, down in the darkness. Little Jimmy didn't really understand it himself. He'd gotten lucky, and gotten rich, and then quit before being lucky wore off. He'd given his pick and his mule away to a newcomer looking to go prospecting, but he kept his pan, since it made a good place to keep bolts and nuts and those little fiddly spare parts that always seemed to need cleaning.

'Morning, Jimmy!' It was Rusty Thomas, who owned the Red Clubs saloon and did all his own distilling. He was pushing a broom around the front porch, cleaning up like everyone else. 'Come in to town for a waker-upper?'

'I've been up since the crack of dawn and you know it, Tommy-boy.'

'Ha! The day you get up before noon is the day you go back under, Jimmy. Stop in and have a drink anyway, on me.'

'Well, I don't mind if I do at that.'

The inside of the Red Clubs was Rusty Thomas' pride and joy. He'd had an artist come all the way from Dos Gauchos, almost a month's ride east and south of Crowdance, to paint the mural behind the bar. Rusty Thomas had decided not to spend any money on getting a mirror, like most saloons had behind the bar, because he only wanted the best for his place and, with rowdy miners around, the mirror would inevitably get broken. The artist had worked for almost a week just to do the first part, then had hung around long enough afterwards to make a couple of changes when everyone saw what he'd painted.

Little Jimmy let his eyes adjust to the dim interior of the Red Clubs and contemplated the mural. It was a masterpiece, if he did say so himself. The artist had done a fine job. On the wall was a perfect reflection of the interior of the Red Clubs, down to the Super Express shotgun that Rusty Thomas kept behind the bar. And to that day, the Painter's Mirror, as it was known, had never been broken. Not even a shot fired in its direction. If ordinary saloon mirrors attracted heavy objects and gunfire, this mirror seemed to repel it. It looked like silvered metal, but Little Jimmy had gotten to touch it, and it felt just like the plaster it had been painted on.

'You really love fine art, don't you, Jimmy.' Rusty Thomas slid a rag along the bar, even though it was already clean, as he watched Little Jimmy contemplate the mural.

'Nah. I only like it because I'm on there.'

'Ha. Your square phiz doesn't deserve mention. I still don't know why I let you in that picture. But enough about your ego . . . what'll you have for that raging thirst?'

'Black Sparkler?'

'Done. Just give me a second.'

As Rusty Thomas began to rummage around for the ingredients, Little Jimmy contemplated his picture in the mirror. It'd been painted years ago, when he was younger, but not too much had changed. His face had weathered well, and although his features were not so sharp as they once were, he still looked like a solid slab of miner. There was a fizzing sound, then a flash of light as the lit match met the fumes from the drink, and then one of the house specials of the Red Clubs slid a few feet down the bar into Little Jimmy's hand.

The tall mug was filled with a dark mixture, made from several of Rusty Thomas' own liquors plus some secret concoction which was kept behind the bar in unlabelled bottles and only used for the Black Sparkler and its cousin, the Red Sparkler. Whatever was in it reacted to liquor pretty well, creating a shooting jet of gas that could be lit on fire and a snappy popping sound. Little Jimmy capped the glass with one hand, putting out the fire, then picked up the mug and took a sip. Cold, but not too cold, and with a slick aftertaste that caught the odor of burning and held it in the mouth for a while. The stuff popped and fizzed even as it went down. It was quite a drink. Little Jimmy sipped another mouthful of the drink, then put down the mug. 'You expecting any mail in tonight's run?'

'No. I gave up on getting that player-piano repair kit. I'm going to write them a letter and get my money back.'

'Are you still on about that? It's been almost six months. They won't do anything for you now.'

'They will if I write them a letter!'

'Tommy, you've got a lot of faith in letter-writing.'

'Hey, just because you never had to doesn't mean it can't help me.'

'Don't let me stop you. But you'd better get writing . . . the mail run will be here in six or seven hours for the ore.'

'Nobody's going to be in today anyway, I've got time.' Rusty Thomas began to polish the bartop out of habit, pushing a damp rag along the varnished wooden countertop in lazy circles. The dark, knotty wood was polished to a dull shine and helped take the edge off the harsh light from outside, working with the burgundy-red walls to make a big change from all the many shades of brown which otherwise decorated Crowdance. There was sand, and dust, and dirt, and even weathered-board brown scattered all around the town, but very little actual color.

'Yeah. That's one thing all of us have here. Time.' Little Jimmy took another sip of his drink and rolled it around in his mouth. He sat in silence, perched half-on and half-off a bar-stool, one leg propped up on the nearest brace of the stool, and the other flat on the ground.

Several minutes passed as Little Jimmy sipped on his drink and Rusty Thomas polished the bar. They'd known each other for years, having both arrived in town before it ever got started and passed the time between then and now getting to be fixtures in the small but growing town. It was a quiet life, except when the mines emptied, but it left plenty of time to think and to do whatever a body felt like next.

✻

Little Jimmy spent most of the afternoon in comfortable silence, nursing drinks along and looking at the people painted in the mirror. Some were old friends, some were people he didn't like so well, and most of them were gone. It was kind of strange to think about, but he always found himself considering where everyone went when he looked at the Painter's Mirror. Some had died. Their parts just stopped working, worn out with age. Most of that was before they had gotten a good doctor in town, though. Others had died in fights, all torn up by gunfire or filleted on the point of someone's knife. Even death to that sort of thing was harder now. The town doctor was a hard worker and smart. Anything that didn't hit the skull or something else equally vital could probably be fixed with enough time. The town graveyard wasn't very full, and even if it had been fuller, Little Jimmy wouldn't have missed those planted there.

The ones that left, though, they were another story. You could always visit the dead, and talk to them, even if they couldn't talk back. Sometimes it was better that they didn't, depending on the person and what you were saying. But those who just left, who went somewhere beyond the horizon and didn't say where . . . Little Jimmy missed them. Some of them were real characters, like Tin Pot Tess, who'd carried the biggest derringer anybody'd ever seen. She hid it in her cleavage and nobody noticed it until she pulled it out to shoot somebody. She'd left early one morning, just packed a bag and started walking. That had been six years ago. Larry Weiss had blown into town one morning with his suitcase full of magic tricks and set up shop on the street corner between Sadler's store and the Robinsons' house. He had spent three months showing off every trick anyone could think of, teaching the kids how to walk coins along their knuckles and palm playing cards. Nobody was quite sure why. Everybody liked him, though, and it was a shock when one morning his little stand was gone. Larry had done a real vanishing act.

Diamond Allen had worn diamond studs in a leather band around his hat. He'd pull one off every night and give it away, just tossed it to somebody at random. He had never seemed to run out of diamonds. He had played dominoes all night long, with anybody that would sit with him. One evening he had set his dominoes all up in a line, put his hat on the chair, and walked out of the Red Clubs. They said he'd walked down Main Street, nodding and helloing as friendly as you please, and then left town heading for the mountains. He hadn't taken anything with him.

'Say, Jimmy. You want to have a hand of cards?'

'Hmm?' Little Jimmy shook his head, chasing away the cobwebs from his mind. 'What?'

'I said you look bored. You want to have a hand of cards?'

'What, you want to lose the Red Clubs to me again?'

'Hey, I know you cheated the last two times, you bum!' Little Jimmy had won ownership of the Red Clubs twice in card games with Rusty Thomas, and twice he'd sold it back. He didn't need to own a saloon, although he'd tried running the place for a bit the first time, just to see how being a respectable businessman felt. It was too much work and too little fun.

'I didn't have to cheat. I just had to let you cheat. You just can't seem to get the counting part right, Tommy.' Little Jimmy grinned. 'Remember, I've seen your book-keeping.'

'Hey, at least I keep books. There's an idea: why don't we get the doc over for a third player? I know he can't be up to much right now. School's let out, so he's done with trying to teach the kids about their Maker.' Rusty Thomas tossed a rag over one shoulder and then slid the chairs back around the last table he'd cleaned.

'Doc's not much fun, Tommy. I reckon he's gotta loosen up a bit before he can enjoy a game of cards.'

'Nah, he played a few hands last week with me when he closed the school for Miss Loretta's birthday. Her parents invited him to the party, but he doesn't get along so well with her dad, what with him being the one who slugged the doc and called him all those names when the doc wouldn't fight back.'

'Just because he plays doesn't mean he'll have any fun with it.'

'He played a pretty good hand, Jimmy. What, you scared that this time I'll do the winning 'tween you and me?' Rusty Thomas winked. 'I'll get him.'

✿

About fifteen minutes later Rusty Thomas pushed one of the swinging doors open and behind him was Doctor Eliott Penn, generally called Doc, since that was the quicker.

He was new in town as people went, having arrived in Crowdance about eight months ago. He was kind of tall but pretty skinny, with a long and lean face that could have been sharpened to a good imitation of a splitting-wedge with a lot of work on a grindstone. His arms were as long and thin as the rest of him, but his hands were quick and sure. If Rusty Thomas was right about him loosening up enough to play some cards then he'd probably be pretty good. Little Jimmy didn't really like the doctor much, but he was willing to allow that the doctor was very good at the two jobs he did: fixing droids up when they got hurt and teaching the kids of the town. Two jobs Crowdance had needed someone to do for a long time.

The doctor wore a natty sage-green string tie: he was always well dressed, though it was all a bit too fancy for Little Jimmy's tastes. 'Afternoon, Doc.'

'Good afternoon, Mister Shaw.'

'How many times do I have to tell you? Call me Jimmy.'

'Right.' The doctor looked around. 'Well, I heard someone say something about a game of cards?'

'You certainly did, Doc. Let me get a pack. You want something to drink? Jimmy, can I freshen your drink up?'

'Yeah, go ahead, Tommy. Give it a bit more fizz.' Little Jimmy left the mug on the bar and his perch on the stool, joining the doctor at a table. Rusty Thomas bustled around behind the bar for a minute, then came out around front, three mugs in his hands which he set on the table. He pulled a new pack of cards out from the front pocket of his apron and set them on the table, then sat down.

'Who deals?'

'You can have first deal, Doc. I'm just having a lazy afternoon.' Little Jimmy produced a match from the band of his hat and lit it, one-handed, against the tip of his thumb. He held it out between two fingers over the drink, which caught promptly and flared up. 'Just relaxing after the exciting times we have here every so often.'

'Too exciting. I'm running low on spare parts and good quality solder.' The doctor flipped open the pack of cards, slid them out, and stripped out the jokers from the bottom and the top of the deck. 'The last batch I ordered had a couple of bad spools and I don't trust it.' He shuffled the cards loosely in his hands a few times, then squared two cuts up against the table edge and riffled them together.

'I guess you'll have to send out an order in a couple of hours, then.'

'I've already got one waiting. I can use the bad stuff if I have to, but I don't like it. I don't think it'll hold well.'

'See, Tommy? That's how you're supposed to handle things going wrong. Prompt responses!'

Little Jimmy grinned at Rusty Thomas as he picked up the cards, inspected his hand, then put them down on the table and used his hand to stifle the flame from his drink so that he could take a sip. The doctor sat and organized his hand, shuffling the cards around and fanning them out, then he slid them back together and set his hand down. Tommy glanced at his hand briefly, then squared them all up, put his cards back down and took a long swig of drink from the mug he'd put in front of his seat. Probably his own homebrew: that was why he'd gotten into this business in the first place. That and his being a bit claustrophobic, which was a problem down in a mine.

'Ha. You wouldn't know a prompt response if it bit you in the ass. Let's keep this game friendly, just pocket change.' Rusty Thomas rooted around in the main front pocket of his apron for a second, then pulled out a handful of change and let it rattle on the table as he set it down. He slid the coins around, then pulled out one and sent it sliding into the center of the table, followed by two cards, face down. 'I'll have two.'

They played casually, the rattle of cards against table as whoever was dealer for the round shuffled punctuating the quiet atmosphere. Rusty Thomas and Little Jimmy left their coins in heaps, sorting out what they wanted when it came time to bet, while the doctor made neat piles of his, stacking them up according to size, largest up to smallest diameter, in little conical stacks.

They talked about recent events, about the new seam in the Mac-Donald mine, about the collapse of a section of canyon wall onto the track leading to the Jones place, and about how many people had gotten to spend some quality time under the doctor's watchful eye because of the new gun the youngest Charles boy had come to town with. They said his daddy'd bought it for him as a birthday gift, since he was old enough now, and had earned it keeping the shipments on time from the mines.

They talked about old times, about when a trio of very unsavoury and slightly deranged drifters had ridden into town, and about the hole that one of them had put in Little Jimmy's side during a fight. The doctor asked about the scars left on Rusty Thomas' otherwise polished head and got to hear the story about the woman in the long coat who'd walked into the Red Clubs one day and tried to kill Rusty Thomas. Every time he told that story what she'd been wearing underneath the coat got a little skimpier and the sword got a little bigger and Rusty Thomas did a little more fighting than he'd actually done. Everybody in the bar had pitched in to save their barkeep, since he was known for rounds on the house and for brewing it as stiff as you asked for. The woman hadn't stopped fighting until they took her apart. The doctor didn't say much about his old times, just that he'd been to school, and worked in a bigger town for a while before moving out to Crowdance.

After a while they noticed it was getting dark. Rusty Thomas glanced at his latest hand, then at the dwindling pile of change in front of him, and tossed his cards in. 'I'm out for this round. You play it out while I go light the lamps.' He pushed his chair back and it scraped against the floorboards, loud in the quiet.

Rusty Thomas went behind the bar, next to where he kept his shotgun, and produced a long, slim wand with a bulbous grip. He adjusted a small knob just above the grip, then lit a match and held it to the stream of gas, lighting a bright flame on the end of the wand. He shook out the match, then turned the knob back some, lowering the flame. The barkeep proceeded to light the lamps behind the bar and then worked his way around the rest of the place, trimming wicks with the pair of scissors he kept in one of the small pockets on the inside of his apron.

With the inside of the Red Clubs lit up, Rusty Thomas shut off the little wand and reached over behind the bar to slide it back inside its cubby. He turned to the game, then looked back at the bar. 'Huh. That's odd.'

'What is?' Little Jimmy looked over at his old friend.

'I was just looking at my clock. It must be wrong. Either of you have the time?'

Little Jimmy shook his head — he didn't carry a watch — but the doctor patted his pockets for a second and then said 'I do.' The doctor pulled out a pocket watch from his vest pocket, popped it open and ran a thumb over the face. 'It's a quarter past seven.'

'That's funny.' Rusty Thomas paused for a moment, then shook his head. 'It is wrong, but it's about twenty minutes slow. I wonder, did we miss the mail run?'

'Nah, it's just late. Believe me, we'll hear them when they get here.'

'Well, even if it is late, so's my dinner. You two want something to eat?'

'I wouldn't say no,' Little Jimmy said, as the doctor nodded and added, 'Please.'

Rusty Thomas walked back through the door beside the bar and into the kitchen. Little Jimmy and the Doc could hear him talking to himself as he rattled pots and pans and fired up the oven with a couple of fresh logs. They waited and made small talk, Little Jimmy asked the doctor about his work teaching the kids and listened to a few stories about how classes were going. After about twenty minutes the door to the kitchen opened again and Rusty Thomas came out balancing three plates piled high with food. He wasn't much of a cook, definitely not as good at it as he was at bartending, but it was solid food, traditional greasy fare, and it filled a body up. That was really all anyone wanted. The three of them tucked into their meal, cards put aside until dinner was through. They none of them rushed the meal, since they were in no hurry. If any visitors came in it would be a surprise, and neither Little Jimmy nor the doctor had anything official to do in the evenings.

✱

It was about half past eight when they all finished. The doctor was just getting up, fork and knife in one hand, plate in the other, when Rusty Thomas said 'Don't worry about moving them, Doc. Just push them to one side. I'll do the dishes before I go to bed.' He gestured for the doctor to sit back down.

'You sure? It's no trouble for me to run them in.'

'I'm sure. Sit back down. Besides, I want as much time as possible to win some of my money back off you two.'

'Good luck.'

'Quiet, you. It's your turn to deal, so deal.' Little Jimmy pushed some sauce around the plate with a knife, then put the knife down and slid the plate across the table to join Rusty Thomas' and the doctors'. He took up the deck of cards, now well broken in, cut them, and riffled them together at the corners.

He was just dealing when the sound of footsteps on the porch outside caught his attention. Little Jimmy turned to see who it was that was coming over, surprised that anybody who was left in town would stop by the Red Clubs, especially at this hour. Over the swinging doors, though, he saw a stranger. The man was fairly tall, and pretty broad as well, and didn't look like the type from anywhere nearby.

He pushed open the door and Little Jimmy could see that he definitely wasn't from around Crowdance. He was built long and skinny, almost like a wedge pointing down. His long coat only accented the narrowing of his body and the two long pistols riding on his hips didn't help it any. He wore a grey hat, brim turned up on one side and left down on the other. He was wide through the cheekbones and narrow through the chin, and when he spoke his voice was kind of raspy and a little high. 'Evenin'.'

'Howdy, stranger.' Rusty Thomas put down the hand of cards that Little Jimmy had reflexively dealt and stood. 'Looking for a drink? We got all sorts here.'

'Nah. Thanks. This place called Crowdance?'

'Yep. This bit of it in particular is called the Red Clubs, though. You been looking for Crowdance?'

'Yes.'

The stranger didn't say anything else. Rusty Thomas walked over to behind the bar, taking his and Little Jimmy's empty mugs with him. 'Well, you mind if I ask why?'

'I got a letter here for Crowdance.'

'A letter? For a town?' The doctor sounded curious. He was sitting half turned in his chair, one arm resting on the back, the other sitting on the table, tapping his cards with one finger.

'That's what it says.'

'Can I see it?'

'This town got a mayor?'

'No. Not really anybody elected around here. We never needed government much. People just sort of take care of themselves.' Little Jimmy spoke up at last.

'Then I don't care who sees it. Here.' The stranger pulled out a large envelope, regular letter size but fairly thick, and walked over, holding it out to the doctor.

'Thanks.' He inspected the front of the envelope, which was addressed with just one word, 'Crowdance' and nothing else. Not even a stamp or a postmark. He turned the letter over, slid one finger under the flap, and pulled it up. The letter inside was several sheets of paper long and folded over several times. The doctor unfolded the letter and inspected the first page. Little Jimmy read over his shoulder as he scanned the letter.

Dear Citizens of Crowdance, it began. *We, the people of Upper Missoulah, feel we must take this occasion to write to you and tell you of what has happened recently in our town. We regret that we may be a little late getting to your next ore shipment. . . .*

The letter went on to tell of the gradual breakdown of daily life as the infrastructure of the town stopped working. Shipments came late to the stores, then they didn't come at all, and the stores had to close. The refinery broke down several times and they tried to repair the broken parts at first, then realized they couldn't make the ones they needed. They sent off for new parts, but each time they fixed the plant something new broke. There were names and dates and then, on about the third sheet, whoever was writing the letter started having trouble writing. First the punctuation became less regular, then the paragraphs ran together, and then finally, on the fourth sheet, the words stopped and the whole page was just covered in numbers. It was like that for three more pages.

'Where'd you get this letter, mister?' Little Jimmy was a little confused, and very suspicious. The letter was just plain strange and the stranger carrying it didn't lend it any credibility. If this was true . . . what was going on? Where would their ore go? It had been hard enough to find a buyer for the raw ore in the first place, and to find another, after they'd been dealing with the same one for years . . . that was not something Little Jimmy wanted to contemplate.

'From the town that sent it. I was passing through as they left.'

'You mean to say they did what they said here, that they packed up and left?' The doctor didn't sound any more trusting than Little Jimmy did.

'Yep. They just packed up and left.'

'What town, Doc? Who's the letter from?' Rusty Thomas came back out from behind the bar, drinks refilled for himself and Little Jimmy.

'Upper Missoulah,' he replied.

'Hang on, isn't that the town with the big refinery? That's where our ore goes, I think.'

'Yeah. It is. Well, I guess the mail run will know what's going on.'

'It's pretty late, Jimmy. I wonder if something happened.' Rusty Thomas sounded a little worried.

'Look, mister. I gotta tell you. I don't know where your mail comes from, but if it came the way I did, it's not coming.'

'What?'

'Every town I've ridden through for the past few days has been the same. Empty. Big or little. One or two of the houses I saw out by themselves had lights, but everything else was dead quiet.'

'What are you saying?'

'That whole towns are gone. I don't know. I don't like it, but I never been this way before and all I know is what I see.' The stranger took off his hat and laid it on the table. 'I'm just glad to find a town with somebody in it is all.'

'Look, stranger. I hope you don't mind if we find your story hard to believe.'

'Believe what you like. Barkeep, I think I will have a drink. Something strong, serve it straight. Whatever you've got.' Rusty Thomas went back over behind the bar, the stranger following, sorted out a glass, and poured it full. The stranger took it and downed it in one shot, then set it back on the bar. He shook his head. 'I don't know what it is. These towns just emptied out.'

'Listen, stranger, why don't you sit down for a bit. Doc, can you make anything out of that letter? Something wrong with the writer or something?'

'I don't know. It doesn't look like much of anything. And I wouldn't know how to diagnose anything without at least hearing the patient's symptoms.'

'They didn't seem to have anything wrong with them that I could see. They could all walk straight and talk straight, or at least they did when I made them answer. They didn't talk any otherwise, though. They just all up and walked right out of town, right as I was coming in.'

'Really?'

'Yeah.' The stranger downed half of the next drink Rusty Thomas brought him and set the glass on the table, then pulled up a chair. 'I never seen anything like it before. And then afterwards, every time I rode through an empty town, all I could picture was those people I saw leaving that town.' He paused for a second to knock back the rest of his drink, then put the glass down and toyed with it. 'I gotta tell you, it kind of scared me.'

'Why? Were they all toting guns?'

'No. Because they weren't carrying anything.'

'That's not so scary to me.'

The newcomer just gave him a look. 'You ever seen a man walking, in the middle of no-where, carrying nothing?'

'No.'

'Well, that's because it doesn't happen. If you're out in the middle of no-where then you're carrying something. Now. Take what doesn't happen, carrying nothing in no-where, and make lots of people do it.' He paused, and looked at his empty glass, and held it up for Rusty Thomas to refill. 'Now, make these people all different sorts of people. Some are big, some are small, and so on. You've got young kids and old geezers side by side, walking, in a big, spread out crowd. But get this. Mothers ain't with their kids. Brothers ain't together. Nobody in that great big crowd is with anyone else. Even though they're all there together.'

'That sounds weird.'

'That is weird.' Rusty Thomas handed over the glass, full again, and this time set a bottle down by its side. 'How could you tell?'

'I don't know. It didn't look like a crowd, though. Nobody seemed to pay any attention to anyone else, or even any one thing in particular. A crowd will stare at something. These people were staring at nothing. And that's another thing. Later, I was riding along, and my horse started to limp on me. I checked and found the old girl'd thrown a shoe. Next town I came to I figured I'd stop and get one put on, or if it was empty like the others, I'd put one on myself.'

'Yeah, and what happened?'

'Strangest thing. I ride into this little town, and like the two before it, it's empty. I'm still thinking about those people I saw leaving Upper Missoulah and so I'm a little spooked. I ride down the main street, look around, and I spot the stables.' The stranger poured a drink for himself, mostly full, with a none-too-steady hand. 'I ride over, since I figure the smithy will be there.'

'Nothing wrong with that.' The doctor began to re-stack his coin towers, knocked over when the table was jarred by the stranger's knee as he sat.

'Yeah. I get around back of the stables and all of a sudden I hear a noise. A 'clink' sound. And then I hear some more, like somebody's banging on a piece of metal. Now I'd swear this town is empty, so I'm about ready to high-tail it out of there. I get ahold of myself, though, and I ride on up, my horse couldn't take going too much further without all four shoes. She'd lame up quicker than y'could spit, then I'd be walking. Well, I get up to the entrance and there's a man in there, and he's bangin' on a wagon wheel, trying to put on a new rim.'

The stranger paused to sip down half his drink. He topped it back up again as he continued. 'I tip my hat back and say "Howdy, stranger. You the blacksmith?" and he nods yes. He looks a little tired, but it's a hot day and working next to a fire all day will tire anybody. So I say, "My horse has thrown a shoe, can you put a new one on her?" and he just looks at me for a few seconds, then all of a sudden he ain't looking at me any more, though his head ain't moved. He just drops his hammer, like he forgot his hands were holding anything, and starts walking.' The stranger stared off into the distance, watching his memories again. 'It was just like those people I saw leavin' that other town, Upper Missoulah. I never heard of anything like it until I ran across those towns.'

Little Jimmy took a turn at the altar of memory himself as what the stranger described rang a few bells. He said simply 'I've seen that once before.'

'Yeah. I don't want to see it again.' The stranger sipped his drink, then decided he'd rather just down it. Little Jimmy watched as he looked at the bottle, wrapped a hand around its neck, started to pour, and then just swigged from the bottle. He set the bottle back down, then reached for it again and repeated the process. 'I just want to stop thinking about it for a while.' His words were slurred and he set the bottle back down with a clank.

Everyone sat quietly as he kept drinking. Then, when he set the bottle down about half finished, Little Jimmy reached across and took the bottle, and then a drink. The stars outside crept out from behind the clouds and sparkled hesitantly over Crowdance, as inside the Red Clubs the four men tried to drink away an image of silent exodus.

My Brother's Keeper

Robin Kate Harding

THREE DROIDS WALK INTO A MECHANIC'S. NO JOKE.

There's a bit of confusion in the doorway, somebody's leg gets mixed up in somebody else's camshaft and then someone else falls over the whole damn mess, it's almost comic – but no one laughs. No one's in the mood today, not with the echoes of last week's disaster still shaking their cogs. There's a lotta good droids who ain't ever gonna be laughing again, and it's making the whole town quiet.

The tangle sorts itself out and Ben comes clattering towards me.

'See, still got tha' damn balance problem Ah tole ya 'bout, Mick. Been in more scrapes 'n' falls this week than Ah been in any other three months outta ma whole life!'

'Yeah, can see that, Ben.' I wave the old droid over to a corner of the workshop where one of my boys is waiting for him.

'Reckon the whole town can see that, Ben,' grouches Jake, as he shuffles past under the weight of a box of spares.

Week ago that woulda been a joke, an' Jake woulda been grinning as he said it. But then again, week ago Old Ben didn't have a balance problem. And he was one of the lucky droids. One of the ones who'd been coming up on the end of the dayshift, when Skippy's crew drilled through to a patch of gas down shaft 23, and sent the whole kit and caboodle sky high. Ben only got hit by the tail end of the shockwave. Put his centrifuge out, sure, but he ain't a heap of cooling slag under a couple of tons of mountain. And that's only a good thing, in my book. I give Jake a glare as he heads through to the back. I know he's hurting over the whole deal, an' more'n most, but that don't give him the right to be ornery with paying customers.

I look over to the door and fix the last of Old Ben's 'victims' with a questioning glance.

'Just a shine, thanks,' says the droid, when he sees me looking. It's the cheapest thing on the menu and pretty much considered a polite way of saying 'Just let me hang around and listen in on all the gossip'. Kid might as well just paint 'New In Town' on his frontal unit. Not that that's a bad thing, at the moment. Rumour has it that we got a few job openings since last week.

*

It's a quiet day, an' I'm curious, so I serve the kid myself. Perks o'bein' the boss, eh? I grabbed a rag an' a tin of Aten and stepped over to him. He gave me a distracted smile, an' made like he wasn't tryin' to look over my shoulder at all that was going on. Polite kid.

'Come from far, have ya?' I asked him, as I smoothed polish over his front. Good workmanship, I thought. You could barely see the join — which my old dad used to say was a sign of true dedication — though it ain't always the best thing, damned hard to get into if ya need to; and there's an old tale 'bout a droid who went mad tryin' to make his children perfect, an' ended up dressin' a piece of sheet metal and carryin' it with him everywhere. Which jus' goes t'show ya.

'Yeah,' answers the kid, in a voice that makes him seem near as distracted as me. I give him a kinda-not-really-accidental nudge, and he snaps back to it. 'Yeah, pretty far. From up near the Basin, past Iron Fall.'

'Din't know there were any droids still livin' up there.'

'There ain't. Not any more.' We both go silent. I get the feelin' this is a tender subject. There's jus' the swish of ma cloth over his limbs for a while, an' then he decides to put me outta my misery.

'Me and my father were the last there.' I decide to take that as an openin' to nosy.

'So, now you're here.' He gives me a nod that I din't really need. 'An' yer pa?'

'He's gone. For nearly a year now — I've been travellin' for nearly that long.'

'Shakin' the dust o' the Basin off your treads, eh?' I ain't never been out that way, but I hear tell it's a pretty bad place to be stuck, if ya ain't got no one to share it with.

'Nah, it's not like that. I'm lookin' for someone - my father's eldest.' He stops, maybe seein' how this sounds a peculiar way a puttin' it. Then he looks up at me, shy like, but serious as a preacher. 'I wasn't yet built when most of the family left to go their own way, so I never met the eldest. I'm makin' my way round to tellin' them all about the death of our father. Just one left now.'

'Huh.' Not much a body can say to that. 'Cept maybe: 'So how many's in this family o' yours, if it's taken ya a year to track 'em all down.'

'Eleven, sir.'

Pheew. Nearly a whole dozen. That's . . . well, that's nothin' shorta impressive. Big families ain't the usual round here. Not round anywhere, I was thinkin', but I've been wrong before now, an' I'll be wrong again, I've no doubt. Don't reckon anyone round here's got the materials for a venture that size. Production like that's the kinda thing ya hear in old tales about the City.

He musta heard the low whistle I give on hearing the number, and he ain't too surprised at my surprise. He looks me full in the faceplate an' grins. I'd a been fine if it weren't for that. I mean, yeah, it's a strange tale and ya gotta admire a droid that's got that kinda dedication, but I got things to do, folks to polish. Got no time for anyone else's quest. But that grin could damn well charm ore outta the rocks.

Now I got a fair appreciation of a finely turned-out droid, but a life in the repairs trade tends to make you wary of such things. When you've seen what's on the other side o'that pretty face plate, it ain't always so pretty, know what I mean? But I get the feelin' I coulda sat down with his blueprints for an armful o'days an' I'd still a been bowled over by it. I guess if your old dad's had that much practice he's gonna get it pretty right near the end.

So, we ended up keeping him round 'til the end of the day, though that came pretty quick seein' as we weren't busy. Him jus' keeping outta tha way, an' sharing some tales 'bout places we ain't never seen, me hopin' no one could see I'd been dazzled by a bot barely made. Luckily, he told a good tale — kept his audience entertained, 'specially with him flashin' those grins — so no one got to questioning me 'bout goin' soft.

'Come on, kid. Let's show ya where the fun happens in this one cog town.'

My second — Morn — she's a cheerful soul an' she grabs him an' wheels him out the front while I shut down shop. By the time I'm round there they've picked up with a round a teasing that's fair to set the poor droid's panels overheatin', but he's takin' it with good grace.

*

Takes it with jus' as much grace when we all drag him round to the Rusty Bucket, which serves us well as our pub, an' dancehall, an' all round good time place. Lizzy, the ole gal who runs the place, eyes us over her row of glass polishers with a mix of interest an' suspicion. Not surprisin'; been a while since we had a new kid in town, an' the last couple we did have weren't worth the time it took to serve 'em. But I give her a nod to let her know I think this kid's a goodun, an' she relaxes back in her seat behind the bar.

We keep the kid in there talkin' 'til well past the time when all good droids should be abed. Turns out he's interested in stickin' around for a spell, earnin' himself some coin, an' maybe putting out some feelers t'see if anyone's heard word of his kin. So we spend the night feedin' him the gossip, an' the local booze, an' I even put in some sensible advice about where a droid who's newly set up might look for work. But eventually Lizzy's makin threatenin' grindin' noises, behind the bar, an' we make our way out inta the starry night.

*

I see him in there the next day making enquiries with all the right droids; nice to know someone round here listens to me. He sees me at the back an' makes a point a comin' over with a drink for us both. Which is a pity, 'cos I couldn'ta been in a worse mood for exchanging niceties if I'd been specially built for the purpose.

He puts the cup down in front o me, an' sits down on the other side all meek like. Guess he can see that somethin's up. Sharp kid: better watch out or he'll cut himself.

'Afternoon.'

Not sharp enough to leave me alone though.

'Nice to know you can take the time out ta come an' see an old boy like me. Not a lotta youngsters who wanna spend there time with a crumbly old cogger like me.' Not that I wouldn't ta been jus' as put out if he'd a walked right past me an' my bad mood. It's that kinda mood. He's lookin' at me out the side of his sockets, tippin' his head down as he does, an' I can see I've put the kid off. Makes me feel like a complete pile o'parts. 'Nah, it ain't you, kid. It's ma bad mood I'm takin' out on ya. Got ma bolts screwed in the wrong way.'

His head tips up a bit, an' he gives me a look that makes me feel about two centuries younger than him. One of these days I'll find out how he does that.

'You wanna talk about it, maybe? I ain't doin' nothin' else at the moment.'

And then he lets out that grin.

Damn, but if I ever find his pa in the afterlife, we are gonna have *words*. Probably words like 'How?' an' 'Damn!' an' 'Ya did do it on purpose, right?' I keep remindin' myself that I'm older, an' wiser, an' that it's none of his business, whilst I tell him all about it.

'It's Jake. Ever since . . . well, ever since what happened to his Skippy *happened* it's . . . ah, I dunno, it's soured his oil somethin' fierce.'

'You sayin' he ain't always in such a good mood?' The kid's givin' me a sly look now an' it almost makes me grin back at him.

'Before, well, he was always a bit of a wild card, but his Skippy cooled him down. Turned him around.'

'And with Skippy gone . . .'

'Yeah, an' half the problem's that the whole town knows what he was like, an' we're all just waitin' for him to revert to original programmin'. But he ain't helpin' to disabuse that notion any.'

'Takes time to get over a hurt like that.' My bad mood ain't all gone; an' I give him a look which says volumes about the things I already know. 'Which you didn't need to be told,' he says, an laughs a little, 'but it's true, an' maybe . . . ' Which is when one of Nick's boys comes round to the table an' taps the kid on the shoulder. Seems Nick's wantin' a word with a young upcomin' droid who ain't afraid of the dangers of Blasting Oil.

I choose ta believe that the advice he was gonna give me was somethin' I'd already thought of: makes me feel better.

❋

He's there next week with Nick's crew; bein' bought a round o'Lizzy's Finest for a job well done. He looks like he's 'bout ta bust his boiler with embarrassment. Kid's gotta knack for makin' friends whether he wants to or not, and he definitely seems in thick with Nick's lot. It's good to see 'em all lookin' happy; it's been a black time of late.

It's all going fine as a smooth line, when the kid goes up to the bar for a round. He's grinnin' an' lookin' over his shoulder and so he don't see that there's someone in the queue in front of him. Kris is serving, an' he don't see anyone either, mainly 'cos he's only got eyes for our golden boy there. So Kris serves him without a thought.

An' then there's a crash. Down the other end Jake's just slammed his mug down on the bar top.

'Annnnnny chance o' gettin' some seeerrvice, rou-round here?'

Kris, he ain't impressed. Not like he ain't seen us all in our cups before. Plus, he knows he's got a whole barful of droids that don't wanna see their server scuffed up none. Gives you a lotta confidence, that does.

'What's got your fender bent, Jake?'

'Ai ain't gonnnna play sec-second drill to some out-a-towner's anymore. An' a, ai ain't gonno listen to any a youse sayin' what ya've aaal been sayin', sayin' bout ma Skippy. Ma poor Skippy.'

It's clear as perspex that he's had a couple too many. An' when I say couple, I'm thinking about twelve too many. Jake's a big model, an' for him to be slurrin' out like his voicebox is cracked, well, let's just say that I'm surprised there's anythin' left behind the bar for anyone else to drink.

But he breaks off then, seems t'curl into himself and ya can hear the whole place give a sigh o'relief. Figured thata'd be it then. One o'the bigger boys would drag Jake outta the place an put 'im to bed, we'd all go back to mindin' our own business; no harm done.

Yeah, shows what I know.

'Chel made a move over to him. 'Jake. Honey, ain't no one sayin' any o'that. We've all been givin' you ya space 'cos we were thinkin' ya needed it. We ain't been meanin' to put you out.' Good words, ain't none better for soothing the savage bot, ya'd think. Yeah, guess ya know as much about that as I do, 'cos Jake rose up outta his curl like the head of a pump jack.

'Oh yeah, that right, is it? An' whattad you know 'bout it, hey? Ya no, no goood, two-byte whorin' drill-biter!'

Now I know Jake's sufferin', but that ain't no reason to go losin' all sense o'propriety. And it certainly ain't no reason to go usin' language like that towards a hard-workin' girl who ain't never been nothin' but the soul o'sweetness an' light. As for . . . well, she might be doin' some dancin' that a polite android might not want his old mother to see, but she ain't never done no whorin', to my knowledge. An' my knowledge stretches pretty far in this town.

We'd all seen that he'd gone too far, and was like as not to be goin' farther, and now it was just a question of who was gonna get to him first to toss him out on his axle. From where I was sat I could see Ford an Josh both stirrin' themselves to do the job, and Lizzy herself was movin' round from behind the bar, which just went to provin' how much of a scene poor Jake was makin', 'cos our Lizzy don't leave her post for very much short o'the end o'the world. But I could also see that they weren't gonna make it in time.

'Chel ain't really able to stand up for her own self — 'specially not against a droid the size a Jake — she just ain't built like that. She's all gentle curls an' gyroscopes, an' the only time I had her in the shop I din't know one end of her insides from another they were so complicated. So I was quietly havin' ball-bearings over the thought of havin' to fix her up, an' the thought of what Jake'd be like when he sobered up enough to find out what he'd done.

His big arm came round like a jack-hammer, an' I'm ashamed to say I put my hand in front o'my eyes, so's not to see the carnage. I don't mind puttin' a droid back together afterwards, but I've never had the gears to see the damage done beforehand.

There was a mighty clang. Which gave me a pause, 'cos that most defiantly weren't the sound I was expectin' to be hearin'. I lowered ma hand, an' there was the kid with one of his arms wrapped around Jake's.

'I think you might regret that in the morning, Jake.'

Ma jaw dropped. An' it weren't the only one. The whole place was in shock. I was wishin' I han't put my hand up now, 'cos I'da loved to see how the kid'd moved that fast. Jake weren't in a place where he could be shocked though. He raised his other arm, an opened his mouth. I was half tempted to put ma hand back. But the kid jus' shook his head, an' leaned in close enough to whisper somethin' in Jake's ear.

An' Jake dropped like a bag a bolts.

Only droid I know who could ever drop Jake in a fight was ol' Skippy. An' Skippy'd been built in kinda the same way I expect they build mountains. The kid weren't no skinny thing, yeah, an' he was bigger than me — there's few who ain't — but he weren't no mountain. An' to do it with jus' a word? That I ain't ever seen.

'Chel looks up at him with her big eyes, an' I reckon she's gonna ask what we're all too stunned to. But she jus' looks at him, serchin' like, then says:

'Sonics, right.'

He looks embarrassed. 'Yeah.'

She nods, like that's that; an' this is a new side to our 'Chel here. I knew she did her own repairs, for the most, but I din't realise she knew that much about workings that weren't her own. Hell, I don't know that much 'bout sonics. Though I'm thinking it might be an explanation for the effect o'that grin.

But she doesn't stay to thinkin' for too long. She lays a hand softly on his arm.

'Thank you.'

They're lookin' at each other like time's stopped, an' I'da been loathed to break the moment, but Ford ain't got my gentle sensibilities. He pushes forward an' slaps the kid on the back.

'Damn, that was good!' He steps round them to drag Jake's carcass outside. 'He gonna be ok, right?'

'Oh, yeah . . . it'll just knock him out for the night. You need a hand?' He moves forward to help take the weight, but we all see the grimace that crosses his faceplate.

'You're hurt!' 'Chel calls, an' it's not another ten seconds before she's hustled the hero of the hour outta the bar and down to her place, to tend to his wounds.

Think our boy mighta made another new friend there.

✱

Now, here's what it is about our 'Chel: she's a classy girl. Ever since she came into town ya could tell it. In the way she steps, an' the way she talks, an' even the way she dances, ya just know she's made of a better class of ore than all the rest of us.

A lot a times that kinda thing would annoy a lotta folks. No one likes being reminded they're the bottom o'the pile. But 'Chel, even before she started roughin' up a bit, she never made a droid feel less. She was just too sweet to ever do that, even by accident.

'Course, being that sweet can cause a girl a bit a trouble. An' when she rolled in it was causing her a whole heap o'trouble. When she arrived she was travellin' with this great hulk of a strolling bullybot. Now, he was a droid I wouldn't like to meet if I din't have my boys backin' me up.

How he ever ended up with our sweet 'Chel I'll never know. Like as not he didn't either. But he sure knew he had a sweet deal, an' he liked to show it off at every opportunity. Liked to show off about how loyal she was as well. Never know how a bright girl coulda stayed with a heap a slag like that for so long.

No matter, 'cos we all did our bit to put a stop to that. I know that I could never stand to see a little droid get hit — an' I ain't a patch on what Lizzy thought to it. She's a fierce one when she's roused, and he roused her like a pair o' Class 11 bellows in a blast furnace.

Was pretty damn funny watchin' him get rousted outta town, an' good-riddance we all said. Then we all rallied round to give 'Chel a good home, 'specially Lizzy, whose gotta soft spot for her a mile wild. An' she's been with us ever since.

But, even with us lookin' out for her, boy, has she ever got the worst taste in, erm, 'dance partners', if ya take my meanin'. Even walked out with Jake for a spell, back before his Skippy took him in hand. So if she was takin' an interest in the kid, and he din't look like to turn bad on us, well, I was all for that. I reckon they'd do well together, they both of 'em got a bit a, well; I guess you'd have to call it shine. Yeah, there's a shine about the both of 'em.

Yep, they got my blessin'. Like they care.

❉

I see 'em round a time or two after that, stepping out together, lookin' real cosy. Guess the kid has given up on the idea a lookin' for his kin. Lookin' at the two o'them, I don't reckon he'll be wantin' to move on any time soon. One night I see 'em out, walkin' through the dark streets arm in arm, the last time Jake comes to see me. He's come to tell me he's leavin' town. I ain't all too surprised.

After what happened, an' what nearly happened, in the Rusty Bucket that night, well, Jake ain't been back in there for fear o'what Lizzy'd do to him. He ain't been much of anywhere. Not that he's exactly wanted company.

Las' couple o'days he'd even stopped comin' in to work, an' after that, I'd known to wait for the knock on my door.

'Ah'm goin' out ta the City, Mick. Ah'm sorry to be leavin' ya in the lurch over the job, an', an' . . . An' Ah'm sorry for a lotta thin's. You wus always good ta us, an' Ah kinda forgot that for a while there, but Ah just can't be stayin' here, now.'

'Yeah, I hear ya, Jake, I hear ya. Good luck to ya.'

An' he was off then. I can only hope he did well. Guess there are some things that not even time can heal.

❋

It's not more than a night later, when there's another late night knocker at my door.

'Not that I don't enjoy a visitor or two, kid, but don't ya think it's a bit late for social calls?' But I open the door anyway an' let him in. 'An' I thought you were seein' your 'Chel tonight?'

He starts a bit at that. 'I was.' There's a pause, an' he turns round. 'I'm sorry, you're right, it's late. I'll, I'll go.

'I ain't chuckin' ya out, kid. Nah, I'm just grumpy 'cos ya woke me.'

'I woke you?' He looks heart-broken at the mere thought. I must be getting old if the youngsters think that even one disturbed night's sleep will finish me off.

'It don't matter none. Sit yourself down here, an' tell ol' Mick what's got ya rattled.'

'I'm sorry,' he says again, lookin' at me with his heart in his eye sockets, 'You were the only one I felt I could talk to . . .'

I get this sudden sinkin' feelin' in ma boiler. He was seein' 'Chel, an' now he's knockin' at ma door in the middle o'the night lookin' like he wants to break himself to pieces. If she's broken his heart . . . or if he's broken hers . . . I've got this sudden image of me an' Lizzy facin' off on each other in the main street, arguing over whose favourite is responsible for the break-up.

He starts up again, afore I can get round to imaginin' Lizzy breakin' me into ma composite parts.

'. . . we, er, me an 'Chel were, er, well, we were . . . tonight, we were . . .'

I take pity, it's too painful to watch for long. 'Yeah, kid, I can imagine what ya were gettin' upto with each other tonight.' He's almost pathetically relieved.

'An' then . . . afterwards, she went to sleep.' Well, that's . . . How d'ya break-up with someone if ya asleep? Or they're asleep? 'An' then, when she turned over,' Maybe he pushed her outta bed? Or got cold bolts? 'I saw — I saw her Trade Mark.'

Huh? 'What, ya din't like the colour? 'Cos, kid, I gotta tell ya, that's the lousiest reason to break-up with someone that I ever heard.'

'No! No, it was fine, the Mark, it was beautiful. But it looked . . .' He stopped here, an' picked up his foot in two hands, showin' me the base of it. 'It looked just like mine.'

Ah, snap.

The Price Of Gold

LAWRENCE DUNCALF

THE SUN WAS JUST BEGINNING TO PEEK OVER THE HORIZON BEHIND him as the prospector first sighted the town. From his vantage point atop the shattered mesa to the east of the town, he couldn't help but be surprised and impressed by its reasonable state of repair. The church in the centre was painted white, the first he'd seen in a while that hadn't long ago shrugged off such raiment. In the long but shortening shadows the streets seemed in decent repair, though at this hour everyone was still in their houses. A small oil complex stood beyond it, its dozen or so nodding donkey pumps inert in the dawn but clearly still in use. This was a town that was still thriving, the first the Prospector had seen in a long time. He smirked to himself as he walked down towards the settlement. He suspected this was his lucky day.

✱

Martha Connor was the first to see the prospector. As she left her house and walked towards the saloon, same as she did every day, she glanced wistfully out into the wilderness and stopped. Despite the early hour, the heat was hazing up the landscape, the wind blowing great clouds of dust, but she thought there was someone out there. Sure enough, the hazy form of a stranger strode out of the dust, clearly headed into town. She waited until he got close enough to escape the distorting haze and then moved to greet him.

'Greetings, stranger,' she said as he got within earshot, 'Welcome to Brass Tack.'

The prospector looked at her and strode over. He made strange clanking sounds as he walked, like he had a loose bearing in his legs or needed some screws tightening. 'Well, hello there, young lady.'

'We don't get many strangers round here. Need directions?'

'Maybe. Any hardware stores here?'

'You'll want O'Malley's. Up the street, past the fountain, and it's the shop next to the undertaker's. He runs that as well, and the mechanic's past that. Looking for some maintenance?'

'Nope. Got some hardware to sell.'

Martha perked up. 'Oh, that's grand! We've been running low on some things recently. Enough to keep you running, but some folks round here want to start building families, and we haven't been able to. What kinda stuff you got?' The prospector opened his bag.

'How much o' that stuff you got?'

The prospector gave her a weird smile. 'Lots.'

'Oh, thank the Maker for you, sir!' She wanted to hug him, 'You're just what we need. You find yourself in the saloon any time, you can have a drink on the house. I'm Martha Connor, the barmaid. If you need a room there, I can put in a good word for you with Otis, the landlord.'

'Why, thank you, ma'am. You're very kind.'

❊

George O'Malley stared at it. It sat there, maybe staring back, maybe not. He looked and looked, but it stayed there, relentlessly, daring him to think that it wasn't real.

'This thing real?' he asked the prospector.

'Real as you or I, and probably more valuable.'

When the prospector had walked in to O'Malley's shop, George hadn't known what to think of him. The stranger was dressed in an unusual way, a blue gold-braided frock coat with gold epaulettes and black tricorn. He wore a pair of goggles over the two steam pressure dials on his face: his one eye was on the end of a faintly smoking cylinder near his vocaliser, like a cigar, above a beard of wires, some connected loosely to the torso, others hanging free and moving despite the lack of wind in the hardware shop.

O'Malley picked up the gold nugget and looked at it with his really good eye, his lens zooming in to look at the rock's surface. He stared at it for some time, then placed it delicately back on the counter. Then he got a hammer and hit it. It was real gold, all right.

'And you say you've got more of this stuff?'

'Aye. Much more.'

'In that sack?'

The prospector's face contorted in what may have been an attempt to smile by one who had never seen one to copy. 'Maybe.'

'Hmm.' O'Malley didn't know whether this prospector had been programmed badly or had just developed cognitive errors in the desert heat, but he was sure the gentleman was barmy. 'I'll give you two hundred for this piece.'

'Four hundred.'

'Four! Ha! You can whistle for it, mate. Two hundred and fifty, and not a scrap more.'

The prospector's eye narrowed. 'Done.'

'You have been. Your timing's great. I had Mr. and Mrs. Dowd in here just yesterday looking for some gold wire. Making a baby.'

'Aw, ain't that just sweet,' said the prospector, neither knowing or caring who the Dowds were. 'With all the gold I found, the whole town can hear the clank-'n-clatter of tiny feet.'

'You find it, I'll buy it, Mr . . . I'm sorry, I didn't catch your name.'

'That's 'cos I didn't say it,' replied the prospector, walking out without looking up from his money.

❋

News of the prospector and his gold nuggets had spread to virtually every resident in Brass Tack by the time he walked into the saloon, along with many others escaping the midday sun. He approached the bar and saw the smiling form of Martha again. She was attractive, with eyes of deep blue and the largest pair of oil tanks he had seen in his life poking from under her black dress with calculated provocativeness. She saw him and her steam vents fluttered, the cogs on one side of her head turning.

'Well hello again, sir.' Martha's eyeshields fluttered open and shut as she passed him a glass of coolant, 'On the house, as promised.'

'Thank you, ma'am.' He took the glass and sipped its contents as he glanced around the room. The townsfolk were all gathering, the pastor in the corner talking in jovial tones with the droid playing the piano, their conversation not distracting the droid's twenty fingers that danced across the piano's keys without faltering. A group of oil workers, the black substance staining their overalls and faces, told jokes to each other and swapped anecdotes over drinks in glasses increasingly stained by oil. Couples sat in booths staring lovingly at each other, and it was these who looked most meaningfully at the stranger at the bar. At several tables droids played cards: men, women, men with women on their arms and laps, and even one woman with a man on her lap. The card players sat with grim concentration, trying not to show reactions that their opponents could read, pushing money and taking money, some laughing in victory, others shuffling off in dejected defeat.

A couple, hand in hand, approached him with nauseatingly undisguised happiness.

'Hi. You the guy who brought in the gold?'

He looked at them with very well disguised distrust. 'Aye.'

'We're the Dowds. We're really grateful for the gold. We've been building our baby for months, and now we can finish him.'

'No problem. What's the child's name?'

'We want to call him Alistair. Give us a week to get him working and you can meet him.'

'I'd like that. This is a nice town. Not many places doing as well as you guys.'

'Well, we're lucky enough to live right on top of a big oil deposit. Every month these guys come from a town on the other side of the western hills and pay real well to take some of it away. We used to even sell it to the other towns around here, though that's getting a bit scarce now. The other towns are fading.'

'Aye, it's getting grim. Lot of folks leaving the places their grandfathers built. Some even going back to the City, and you know things are getting desperate when you want to go there. But enough of how grim it is. Who are those guys playing cards?'

'Oh, so you're a gambling man, eh? Best way to get to know 'em's to go play! Just watch out for her.'

Mrs. Dowd gestured surreptitiously to the woman with the man on her lap, a woman with delusions that a new face-plate and voice module could hide that she was nowhere near the age she claimed to be. 'That's Shelley Polterneck. The man on her lap is her husband, Jimmy, and let me tell you she's the brains of the outfit. They make their money in ways the Mayor and Sheriff would love to put 'em in jail for, and you wouldn't be the first traveller to find them unburdening you of your valuables, either at the poker table or in the alley outside. And you'll definitely want to stay away from their two boys.'

Mrs. Dowd made another gesture to two gents at the next table along. One was made of battered and tarnished brass, with two big eyes that narrowed shrewdly as he studied the hapless droid playing cards with him. His brother, sitting next to him, was made of cast iron, heavily built and riveted together like a tank with a scowl. The seat seemed to strain under his weight.

'That's Jake and Pete. Jake's the brass one,' she continued. 'These days they do most of the Polternecks' dirty work. They cheat at cards, steal from everyone, and there are . . . rumours. Every so often someone annoys Ma and Pa Polterneck, and sometimes those people disappear. No-one can prove anything, but . . . '

The prospector's face smiled in understanding. 'Don't worry, ma'am. I'm a big boy: I can look after myself.'

❋

Shelley looked at her cards. He had to be bluffing.

The stranger in the unusual costume had sauntered up to the table and sat down in the seat the newly penniless Bob Hawkins had vacated a few seconds earlier.

'Mind if I join you?' he'd asked.

Shelley had looked him up and down. He didn't know who he was dealing with. 'Sure, stranger . . . if ya got the coins.'

The prospector had made a clanking sound of loose components as he'd dumped a tightly-bound sack next to the seat and sat down. He'd taken his cards and . . . smiled, in a strange and ugly kind of way. 'That was your first mistake,' she'd thought. 'You'll be easy to read. May as well just dump your money and leave.'

Nine hands in, she knew she had underestimated him. She couldn't read his expression: since he sat down all he'd done was keep that ghastly approximation of a smile on his face, never moving his head at all, just the oculator on the end of that smoking rod switching inscrutably between his cards and the players, and speaking in that strange accent of his. Worse, he was winning. He had money in his pockets, he always raised, and more went back in those pockets than came out.

'I raise you ninety.'

Shelley looked at her money. He had taken nearly three hundred from her. Was he trying to get himself killed? She shot a glance to her son Jake. He and his brother gave slight nods back.

'I see your ninety. Hope you ain't wasting my time.'

She put down her cards. Five, six, seven, eight and nine of Cogs. It was always useful having extra cards stashed in Jimmy's sleeves, since ladies' sleeves were not designed with cardsharping in mind.

'Straight flush.' She smiled maliciously.

The prospector looked at her, his gruesome smile not wavering, not moving at all. He slowly brought his cards down and laid them on the table. Shelley's expression faded to one of horrified surprise.

'Royal flush,' the prospector said, rolling the r as his opponent looked at his ten, Jack, Queen, King, and Ace of Pistons.

'You gotta be cheating. I'm the best card player in Brass Tack.'

'You forget, ma'am, that I'm not from Brass Tack.' The prospector leaned forward to collect his winnings, quietly whispering, 'Besides, it looks to me like your husband's sleeve is the best player.'

Both Shelley and Jimmy looked at him in horror. Shelley narrowed her eyes. 'First ya get lucky finding that gold, now ya get lucky at cards,' she whispered, her voice aflame with menace and meaning. 'I think you'd better leave before your luck runs out, if ya get my drift.'

The prospector chuckled defiantly and, stuffing his winnings into his pockets and gathering his amorphous sack, strode off as far as the bar. Jake and Pete, moving almost as one, crept over to their mother.

'Want us to take him outside?'

'Not yet. Wait until he leaves on his own. I bet the gold is in that sack of his. If we get that, we can keep it ourselves and get rich.'

✻

'He's been in there all afternoon,' Pete said a little too loudly. They had stayed in the saloon all afternoon waiting for the prospector to leave, but all he did was drink and talk to the townsfolk and played more cards. When the two brothers had left to wait outside, the sun had already set. Darkness gave them all manner of hiding places to wait for him unnoticed but for Pete's loud voice. 'He's probably got himself a room from Otis and a girl to share it with him. Why don't we go beat up someone else instead?'

'He'll come. Ma said so,' Jake said, crouched with his brother in the alleyway across the street, behind a bin full of rusty debris. Sure enough, after only a few more minutes of waiting, the Prospector staggered clumsily out of the saloon, drunk on cheap coolant, the sack perilously close to being dragged along the ground.

'Now's our chance!' Jake urged his brother and they leapt out from their hiding place. Pete began to close almost instantly, while Jake was slightly behind.

'Ah, let me guess,' the prospector slurred, 'you're the one who thinks he's the smarter of the pair, so you're going to do all the talking, as if I'm meant to be intimidated by you. Meanwhile the anvil on legs here is the one who gets his hands dirty when I inevitably fail to be intimidated. Am I right?'

Jake began to speak, then stopped. 'Well, yeah, that's right. So now you know the deal, hand over your money and that gold of yours and save us some time.'

'Hmm. Let me think about that for a moment,' said the prospector. Without hesitation he lifted his free arm, and with a hiss of steam venting the fist was suddenly propelled on its telescopic arm towards Pete. The point-blank force of the blow knocked the colossus flying, and by the time he realised he was flying he had already landed in the bin of debris. It unbalanced and wobbled for a few seconds before deciding it didn't like the droid and toppled over, dumping Pete onto the ground and the dust.

Jake watched it happen, uncertain as to how to respond. His gaze snapped back to the prospector, whose hand was casually retracting back into the coat's sleeve.

'Hmm. Looks like I'm thinking "no".'

There was a great smash as Pete righted himself and kicked the bin towards the prospector. It flew through the air at least as gracefully as Pete hadn't and hit the prospector square in the face, knocking him over backwards until only a pair of feet poked out from the heap of twisted and rusty metal. The sack dropped the few inches to the ground.

Jake stepped up to the figure under the bin, stooped down and picked up the sack. 'Pete, wanna finish him off?'

Pete rubbed his face. 'I think my nose is broken. Need Pa's screwdriver.' He walked up and gave the prospector a good kick. 'We'll deal with you later.'

✷

The sack was placed on the table in the Polternecks' house. Shelley looked at it, then at her sons. Jimmy was repairing Pete's nose in the corner, but looking over at his brother and mother.

'And the stranger?'

'We'll go back and finish him off once Pete's fixed.'

'Open it. Let's look at the fruits of my labours.'

Our labours, Jake thought, as he opened the sack. He regretted thinking this upon looking into the sack. There was no gold. There was no money. Upon looking into the sack, he deduced with remarkable swiftness that, rather than any of these valuable substances, the object he was scrutinising was without doubt a snake.

An angry-looking snake, with glowing red oculators and a warning notice next to a mouth full of teeth with powerful pneumatic assists at each side. Its jointed sections were edged with yellow and black stripes to emphasise the point. It roused itself from its slumber with deceptive harmlessness, looked up, noticed that the face looking in wasn't familiar, and hissed, gas escaping from its pneumatics, then lunged.

Shelley watched Jake as he staggered back, his face replaced by the writhing sinuous whipping of the long body of the snake. She sighed.

'Jake, that there's a snake.'

A pained whine came from under the snake, which she took to be a gesture of him having noticed this as well. 'Yeah, I guess you can tell that from that range,' she continued, uncaring, 'but I was lookin' for gold. Gold is a rock, remember? It comes in nuggets, and is kinda, well, kinda gold sort of colour. It ain't black and yella, and it don't move, and it ain't a snake!'

Shelley grabbed one of the snake's body segments with one claw and struck Jake's fang-damaged head with the other. The force was sufficient to separate the snake from her son's head, and her son's head from its body, rotating around and around and unscrewing (for such was the method of its attachment) until it ran out of screw and came away.

The head flew across the room and clattered along the ground, skittering under a sofa. Jake's body stood rigid, wondering where the central processor was and why it wasn't making it move any more. Shelley sighed, then turned the snake around to face her, at arm's length of course. It hissed and whipped its ophidian length belligerently, squirming in her steel grip as it tried to repeat its previous success on the new target. Shelley Polterneck simply looked at it, sensing a kindred spirit, alike in their malevolence but herself the superior in terms of intellect and methodology.

She whirled around and battered the creature's head against the door frame repeatedly, the snake hissing great clouds of pneumatic gas and wriggling all the more. Bits of dented and battered plating began to fall, followed by bits of circuitry, springs and cogs. Eventually, the snake still resisting despite being all but wrecked, she hurled it across the room, the mangled machine smashing through the window and landing in the dust outside. It writhed in the dust, barely able to move, unable to move in any particular direction, but still hissing and flailing as much as it was still capable.

Shelley composed herself, fished her son's head from under the sofa, and looked it in the eyes. 'Ya failed me, boy.'

Jake tried to hang his head in shame, but since his head was being held in his mother's claws was unable to do so. He resorted to simply looking down. 'Sorry, Ma. We didn't know.'

She took the talking head over to its body and set it upon the shoulders, screwing it back on. Eventually the body realigned with the head's contacts and sparked back into life.

'Don't worry, son,' said Shelley with all the maternal tenderness of a trash compactor. 'You and your brother will just have to go find the stranger again, and get him to give you his gold. He must've hidden it somewhere. Find out where, or get him to show you: then finish the job and bring me that gold! Jimmy! Have you fixed Pete yet?'

'Yes, dear,' said Pa Polterneck, putting his tools away as Pete rubbed his new nose.

'Don't pick your nose, dear, you'll dislodge a bearing,' Shelley told him impatiently.

'Yes, Ma,' Pete replied, and looked at Jake to see if he was ready to leave. He was already leaving, so Pete hurried after him like a sack of anvils in a washing machine.

✱

The drunken prospector had been in sleep mode, dreaming of a great expanse of oil, deep and broad, with no land on it. He saw himself on top of a machine of girders and steel plate and propellers, floating on the oil and moving around in it. He was an explorer, a dashing rogue travelling that landscape, master of such a domain. He saw another similar craft, and he attacked it, cannon at the side of his floating vessel firing at it, crippling the other vessel so that he could pillage its contents and remain out in this new world where there was no dust or sand, just roiling oil.

He was woken by the bin and rusty debris being lifted from him by a scowling cast iron tank on legs and a brass git kicking him in the chassis.

'I'll call the vessel *The Chrome Corsair*!' he muttered.

Jake stopped and looked at him, confused. 'What?'

The prospector looked up at Jake. 'Never mind. What do you two want now? Was it not enough to steal my snake?' The drunken prospector smiled with malevolent glee. 'How did you get on with my pet? I keep him around for when people try to rob me.'

Pete put a foot on the prospector's chest plate, the sound of metal grinding against metal like mating suspension bridges. 'Ma killed it. We wanna know where you hid the gold.'

'What gold?' the prospector replied, smirking with the malicious mischievousness of the bitterly aged. Pete's foot pressed down harder, and he was rewarded by the needles on the prospector's steam pressure dials flickering anomalously beneath the goggles.

'Oh, that gold,' the prospector feigned remembrance, and slapped Pete's leg to signal he was ready to get up. The foot stayed resolutely where it was.

'You're going to tell us where that gold is, or Pete here's gonna make sure we can sell you for scrap metal,' Jake said in his most threatening voice, or rather his least pathetic voice.

The prospector looked at Pete. Pete looked like he had forgotten that he had his foot on someone and was staring into space waiting for Jake to tell him what to do. He looked at Jake. Jake looked back with the confidence of one used to standing behind someone tough and making disparaging remarks. The prospector sighed. 'Fine. I'll take you to where I hid the gold: but I warn you, it's pretty far away. Better make sure your Ma knows where you're going.'

'She knows what's going on,' Jake replied, and signalled Pete to ease up. The crushing weight on the prospector lifted as Pete took his foot off him, then came back as the oaf grabbed him bodily and manhandled him to his feet.

'We leave at dawn, gentlemen,' he said authoritatively.

'Wrong,' Jake riposted with less authority. 'We leave now.'

'Suit yourself,' the prospector huffed, and turned to the east, walking as if he didn't care if they were following. Jake and Pete exchanged glances and followed him.

❀

'So tell me.' The prospector stopped and whirled around to speak to them, for the first time since they began walking. It was also the first time he had stopped walking. 'What exactly does your Ma think she can do with my gold?'

They were back on the shattered mesa, and the sky to the east was beginning to brighten, though the sun had yet to make its customary daily appearance. Jake and Pete had never been this far from home before.

'She'll do the same thing you did,' Jake replied, uncertain at what the prospector was talking about, 'sell it for money. O'Malley'll take it off our hands.'

'Really? O'Malley knows I'm the one with the gold. If you or your Ma turn up with the gold instead, don't you think he'll get suspicious and let the sheriff know?'

Jake thought about it. 'We'll sell it to the droids from over the hills when they come for the oil. Get a better price for it from them too.'

'Hmm. That's a good answer.'

'Yup. D'ya think we're all dumb as Pete just 'coz we're small town droids?'

'No, but I thought it might have run in the family, since you seem to tell Pete what to do and your ma tells you what to do. So tell me: now your ma's not around to hear you, what are you really going to do?'

Jake looked at him, confused. 'Nuthin' different.'

'Really? Why? With that much gold you and your brother could leave, find a new life in a bigger and better town. What's there for you in Brass Tack 'cept for the droids from the west taking all your oil and your ma telling you how to live your life?'

Jake looked at the prospector shrewdly. 'I know what you're doing. You're trying to turn me against my own ma!'

'Me?' the prospector replied, feigning innocence. 'Now why would I want to do that?'

'I don't know, but I love my ma and she loves me. Same goes for Pete.'

Pete nodded blankly.

'Suit yourself,' the prospector sighed, and started walking again.

❋

The sun had risen and grown hotter, and the prospector had led them into a canyon to escape the glare and the heat.

'What are we doing here, old man?' mocked Jake, 'Afraid of overheating? All that coolant you drank yesterday, you should be fine.'

'Ah, but I am, as you pointed out, an old man,' the prospector replied, 'I can't risk a rivet bursting in the heat. I might never get it fixed, and then I wouldn't be able to lead you youngsters to my gold stash, now would I?'

Jake muttered under his breath, but said nothing loud enough to be heard. He sat down on a rock and laid back. 'Well, if we're resting, I'm gonna get some shutdown time. I told you we shoulda left at dawn instead of right away,' he announced, forgetting that it was he who had insisted on the immediate departure. 'Pete, watch him. Make sure he doesn't try to run away.'

Jake's oculators went dim and blank. Pete watched the prospector, and crushed pebbles in his giant fists to pass the time.

'So, Pete,' the prospector began. *Start out nice and simple, so as not to overtax the droid's processor.*

'What?' Pete replied.

'Don't you think you'd be better off without your ma and pa? All children have to leave sooner or later.'

'I don't wanna,' Pete replied. 'I loves my ma.'

'A-haa.' The prospector stayed quiet for a calculated pause. 'And what about Jake?'

'Jake loves Ma too.'

The prospector could tell this was going to be a rather one-sided conversation. 'Do you think she loves you both back?'

'Yeah.'

Another pause. 'Equally?'

Pete didn't understand. 'Uh?'

'Do you think your ma loves you and Jake equally?'

'I dunno. Why?'

'Well, it seems to me that Jake thinks he's better than you, and he might have picked it up from your ma.'

Pete stood up. 'Jake's my brother! He likes me!'

The prospector shook his head, beard wires flailing. 'No, Pete. Jake treats you like a pet. He thinks you're stupid, and that makes him think you're not as good as him.'

Pete looked down. 'I know I'm not as smart as other people, but I's got good points. Like I can smash things really well!' Pete smashed a really big pebble to prove his point.

'I can see that, and it's very impressive,' the prospector replied, 'but do you think Jake appreciates you as much as you deserve?'

Pete thought for a while. A long, long while. It was clearly a rather difficult process. 'I dunno. He lets me hang around him; the other boys in town ain't like that. But he's always tellin' me what to do! Like I don't have a mind of my own!'

The prospector suppressed the urge to be sarcastic. 'Maybe he doesn't deserve to be loved as much as you, Pete.'

'What you mean?' Pete asked, scratching his head, the two metal surfaces screeching together.

The prospector looked at Jake, who was still asleep, then beckoned for Pete to come closer. Pete ambled closer obediently.

'Pete, is there anything you want to do? What is it that you want to do with your life, if Jake wasn't telling you to do other things?'

Pete made an expression of deep concentration as he tried to think of an answer. 'Well,' he eventually said after such an astonishingly great pause that the prospector had begun to suspect that Pete had forgotten the question and had stopped thinking, 'I like animals. They don't last long around me, 'cos I pet them so hard they break, but if I learned to be gentle like, maybe I could be an animal engineer?'

The prospector steeled himself against the lunacy of what he was about to say. 'You could be an animal engineer, Pete,' he said, barely able to believe the bare-faced cheek of his deception, 'but Jake will hold you back. He doesn't want you to be successful on your own, because he wouldn't like you proving that you are better than him.'

Pete looked at his brother, then back. 'Really?'

'Yes. But—' here the gambit would be tested '—suppose Jake didn't go back to Brass Tack?' Pete looked at him blankly. 'What if you went back to your ma, with the gold, but without Jake. Ma would be so proud of you for bringing the gold back for her, and even more so because you proved that you could be relied upon and Jake couldn't. And then, without Jake, you could be an animal engineer, and no-one would get in your way.'

'But why wouldn't Jake come back?'

The prospector prepared for the big part. 'Because you could kill him.'

Pete's eyes widened in alarm. 'Why?'

'Because he's holding you back. As long as he's around, he won't let you be who you want to be. You'd always be 'Jake Polterneck's brother', never 'Pete Polterneck' in your own right.'

Pete looked at his brother's sleeping form. 'But I like Jake.'

'You don't have to do it now,' the prospector said soothingly. 'It's still quite far to my stash, so ask yourself this: you like Jake, as a brother should, but does Jake like you, or are you just his pet?'

❁

When Jake awoke, he felt refreshed. The sun has passed its zenith, and the air was not feeling as oppressively hot. The prospector's fragile chassis could continue.

'Okay, we've rested long enough,' he announced, standing. He gestured for the prospector to rise and get moving, oblivious to his brother's unfamiliar expression: one of brooding reflection.

'Jake,' Pete asked, 'can't I sleep now?'

'No, Pete,' Jake replied without even looking over, 'we have to get moving. Besides, your processor doesn't work as hard as mine. You don't need to rest.'

Jake pushed the prospector ahead of him, and didn't notice Pete's face as he clanked after them, a face that reflected his poisoned state of mind.

❁

'So how much further's this stash?' Jake asked, as they walked across an apparently featureless expanse of dusty desert dirt. But for the occasional mound of unrecognisable rust that might once have been dead droids of some type or another, there was nothing as far as the oculator could see. The sun was getting low behind them, and their shadows were lengthening in front of them.

'I hid it in an abandoned town. We're not that far from it now.'

'We've only been walking for a day and half a night! I didn't know there was a town this close to Brass Tack.'

'You clearly didn't hear me. There isn't. It's just the ruins of one. Been abandoned for years, probably deserted before you and your brother were built. These days the frontier towns are decaying: mines get depleted, oil reserves dry up, industry grinds to a halt. Some try to carry on in a town, eking out an existence without quite knowing what to do with it any more. Others migrate to other towns, and help shorten their new home's lifespan. Some even get so desperate that they go back to the City. At least one town I know's even taken to becoming an entire settlement of bandits, attacking anything that comes within striking distance and looting it for what they can oil and parts to keep themselves and their Mark Twos going. Brass Tack's one of the lucky towns, though chances are its luck won't last forever.'

'What's this old town called?'

The prospector smiled. 'Yellow Crater.'

Jake was intrigued. 'Why's it called that?'

'You'll find out in about two minutes.'

✿

Jake had to be caught two minutes later as he almost fell off a cliff.

'Presenting the Yellow Crater, with the deceased town of the same name.'

The dust and heat haze had stopped him from seeing it before, but the horizon had been getting closer. It was only as he almost stepped obliviously off the precipice that he could see it. The landscape had dropped off completely, and they were standing at the lip of an enormous crater. It must have been an impressive cataclysm that created it. By Jake's guess it had to have been nine miles wide. The evening sun certainly cast a shadow here: the crater was swathed in shade. The ground was the same material as everywhere else in the desert, but in thousands of places there seemed to be enormous outcrops of bright yellow. In the centre was a town that may once have looked uncannily like Brass Tack, but was now just a collapsed skeleton of structures that had had no-one to maintain them against the ravages of dust storms and the relentless march of time and weathering.

'What's the yellow stuff?' Pete asked as he caught up and looked upon the sight.

'Sulphur,' the prospector replied. 'Might have been under the ground before the crater was formed, then thrown to the surface; either that or the meteor that caused it was full of sulphur.'

'What's a meteor?' Pete had never heard of one.

'It's a rock that falls from the sky. Makes a big impact when one this big hits. It would have thrown so much dust in their air that it would have blotted out the sun, and the shockwave on the ground would have probably destroyed everything for hundreds, maybe even thousands of miles around. It might have even caused this desert to be created.'

'When did this happen?'

'No-one knows. Years before our kind were ever built. It's likely been here so long that the desert has come and gone several times between then and now. Maybe this meteor caused the desert. Maybe it's true that the Maker's industries made the desert again after the land had recovered from the meteor. I doubt we'll ever know, and it doesn't really matter. I hid the gold in that town: that's what matters.'

'Where?' Jake asked impatiently.

The prospector pointed to a rather more graceful ruin. 'In there. The old church. Centre of the town: only place to put something valuable.'

Jake nudged his brother. 'Pete, find a way down.'

'Why me?' Pete groused petulantly.

'Because he's too old and I ain't as strong as you. If we fell down the crater we'd be scrap by the time we reached the bottom. Now go!'

Pete looked at his brother, then stomped off.

The prospector waited until Pete was out of earshot. 'Do you like that oaf?'

Jake snorted. 'I haveta. He's my brother. I can't leave him to his own devices: he ain't smart enough to take care of himself. Do you know he used to say he wanted to be an animal engineer! He can't even stroke one without smashing it to bits, and there's no way he's smart enough to maintain one!'

'So he's a bit of a burden on you?' the prospector asked, hiding his sly grin. This one was going to be a lot easier.

'Ha! It's worse than that! Without me and Ma telling him what to do he'd just sit around smashing things. Sometimes I wish he'd leave. I have my own dreams; I gots things I wanna do without him following me around like a bad smell that breaks everything. You know how frustrating it is to have dreams and not be able to chase 'em?'

'Aye,' the prospector said, wistfully, 'I had this idea for a machine that could float on oil.'

Jake looked at the prospector: *Clearly*, he thought, *this one was a barmy old coot.* 'Yeah, that's exactly what I'm talking about, old man.'

The prospector leaned in closer. 'You know, you could always get rid of him.'

Jake looked at him with a shrewd eye. 'How do you mean?'

The prospector gestured to the landscape. 'Middle of nowhere, all on your own, unknown landscape . . . anything could happen.'

'You mean, I could make anything happen,' Jake replied, catching on to the idea with startling disregard for morality.

'Exactly. You could take the gold back to your ma, and she'd be so proud of you, that you could be relied upon and Pete couldn't. You could even use the gold to help you achieve your ambitions, without your brother tagging along and ruining everything.'

Jake looked at the prospector. 'You're a sly old devil, ain't ya?'

The prospector puffed himself up. 'You need to have a quick processing speed to survive out here on your own. Something, incidentally, which Pete doesn't have. Just think about what I said.'

The prospector wandered off in Pete's direction: he was waving at them to show them the path down he had found.

✻

This was going better than expected, the prospector thought. Every time one brother wasn't looking at the other, the other was making very evil expressions at his sibling. They had stopped even thinking about the prospector, who now sauntered behind them as they walked nervously down the old streets of Yellow Crater Town.

The night had closed in around this town with a certain sinister air. The crumbling buildings loomed over them, casting shadows that danced at the edges of their minds and goaded their paranoia. The slightest creak of an old awning in the wind became the warning of an impending attack by Maker-knows-what. Turning corners required the brothers to steel themselves against whatever unknown horror might be lurking in the darkness.

The prospector found the brothers' fear amusing. He knew there was nothing around for miles, hadn't been since the town died, and if there was anything, the prospector was old and grizzled and wise enough to deal with it. For all their criminal bravado, the brothers had never been so far from what they were used to. In Brass Tack, they were the nasty people lurking in the shadows, they were the ones that people feared. Here, the tables were turned: they didn't know what could be here, and didn't know if they could make it go away if it came to say hello.

They turned a corner and saw the church in its full glory, or steadily degenerating lack thereof. The spire was collapsing very slowly: it was leaning precariously to one side with a pile of already fallen masonry underneath. The windows had long since shattered, and the wind howled through the spaces like someone was using an angle-grinder inside. The giant doorway yawned open like a blasphemous maw pointed right at the three droids, the doors themselves hanging more by the corrosion on the hinges than by the hinges themselves. The walls, presumably once painted white like the church in Brass Tack, was now reduced to a mess of rotting blotchy greys and browns, thankfully reduced to just grey in the gloom.

It occurred to the prospector that being in this town was like seeing the future of Brass Tack: the oil reserves would eventually dry up, as they had been doing all over the frontier desert, and the people of Brass Tack would be forced to abandon their town to this sort of decrepitude or suffer the same fate themselves. But then, he was an old man, and well used to moribund thoughts like that.

'Well, gentlemen,' the prospector announced as they approached the denuded church steps, his voice echoing around in the sepulchral silence, 'Here's the church. The gold is hidden under a loose flagstone in front of the altar at the front. You'll know which flagstone because I've scratched a cross on the surface. X marks the spot, as the saying goes.'

'You stay out here,' Jake told the prospector. 'We'll decide how to deal with you later. Come on, Pete, let's get ourselves some gold!'

The prospector watched as the twosome walked into the church, struggling to conceal their trepidation.

It was black as crude oil inside the church: the moonlight shone as far as the open windows and then seemed to stop, illuminating nothing inside the wreck of a holy place. Jake flicked a circuit in his head, and a panel slid away in his upper chest to reveal two lamps, which switched on and shone two tapering beams of yellow light into the church.

By the Maker, but this place is depressing, he thought.

The interior had fared no better than the exterior. A hefty rafter had fallen and impacted upon the altar with such force that the stone table had been smashed in, like a desecrated tomb. The pews were, at best, pew-shaped piles of firewood: at worst, just plain firewood. Any objects of value had long been removed, either taken by the townsfolk when they left or stolen by passing looters afterwards. A giant mural painted on the far wall, depicting the Maker's Mark surrounded by scenes from holy scripture, was barely recognisable, so much of it had been effaced by age and neglect. A few tattered flags and tapestries remained, but could barely be considered more than simply mouldering rags hanging on poles. The flagstones underfoot were worn and, in some cases, shattered and uprooted. There was virtually nothing that had stared Time in the face and fared well.

Jake walked cautiously towards the slightly raised dais upon which the smashed altar was situated. Pete followed, reluctant to stray too far from the lamps.

'Jake? I don't like it here. Can we hurry up and get the gold so we can go home?'

'Shut up,' Jake responded tersely.

Sure enough, there was a flagstone that looked recently moved, and an X had been carved surprisingly deeply in the stone.

'Pete, you lift the stone. I'll keep the light on you.'

Pete grumbled and clamped his enormous hands around the stone. He lifted it into the air and cast it aside with virtually no effort, impacting with the other stones on the floor several metres away with a boom that reverberated around the church like a thunderclap from the Maker Himself.

Jake peered into the hollow underneath where the stone had been. There was a leather case inside, and a note resting on top. Jake took the note, not intending to read it.

'I've got the gold,' Jake said to Pete. 'Now it's time I got rid of you.'

'No,' Pete replied, 'Now I'm gonna get rid of you!'

'What? But I'm your brother!' Jake retorted, knowing that logic did not have to be used against Pete. The hypocrisy of the riposte wouldn't occur to him.

'Don't matter,' Pete rumbled, 'I don't need you any more.'

'You dang treacherous bastard!'

'Ma's gonna love me like she should, and I'm gonna be an animal engineer!'

Jake dropped the note and took a step back, furious. 'You're just a big dumb brute, and all you're gonna be is dead!'

'I'll kill you!'

'I'll kill you first!'

'Wrong, boys,' the prospector said, immensely pleased with himself, 'I'm going to kill you both instead.'

He put both his hands on a plunger and pushed down. The inside of the church exploded into yellow and white fire, impossibly glaring in the darkness of the night. The church collapsed in upon itself, burying its contents under a hundred tons of stone and wood. A dust cloud smothered the church as the sound of the explosion sundered the air for miles around and the ground shook violently.

Eventually the sound died down and the dust settled. The prospector left the detonator where it was. He wondered if they had read his letter:

Dear Looters,

> *Congratulations on being so thoroughly stupid. You will find the case included with this note is empty. I'm not one for holiness: I've barely set foot inside a church in my life, and I don't see why I would put gold in one. I'm afraid there is, however, one surprise you'll find in here: do you really think I wouldn't booby-trap a place like this? The whole church is rigged with dynamite.*

Ta ta.

The prospector walked into the saloon of the ruined town of Yellow Crater. He sat down at the table in the corner and sat in silence for a while, recovering from the noise of the explosion. The town would never be the same again, he thought with a chuckle.

Eventually he leaned down and removed the floorboards under the table. There was a leather case in the hollow space underneath. He picked it up and laid it on the table, then opened it. It was full of gold nuggets: he had really hit paydirt. He closed up the case and carried it out of the saloon. Should he go back to Brass Tack? The townsfolk wouldn't know where the brothers had gone, and there would be nothing to say that he was connected with their ever-so-unfortunate disappearance. Indeed, the townsfolk would likely thank their lucky stars that the two were gone and not think too deeply about it. All except Ma and Pa Polterneck. No: no longer Ma and Pa, just Shelley and Jimmy Polterneck now. They would know, but without their boys they wouldn't be able to do anything to him. Still, it might be awkward.

The droids from beyond the hills, he thought as he walked through the night breeze. He could intercept the convoy before they reached Brass Tack for the oil run. Get a much better price than O'Malley would be able to offer. Enough money to build his oil-floating-vessel. He would call it *The Chrome Corsair . . .*

Legacy of Life

Nick Westwood

Her vision cleared as if a dust cloud had begun to settle around her, and her neck ached as she turned her head to take in her surroundings. She was in a familiar room, though she couldn't yet place the reason for its familiarity. The chair in which she sat was comfortable but worn, clearly very ancient indeed — as was the droid in the chair on the opposite side of the room. She stood carefully, as it seemed that every part of her ached, and floorboards creaked underfoot as she crossed the room.

She bent to quietly examine the old droid, thinking that he may have been asleep; but instead found no signs of life at all. Just then a thought struck her, and she quickly ran an internal self-diagnostic; the results showed that while her key systems were in good working order, her memory core regulator was in bad shape. At least it was nothing life-threatening, but she resolved to get it replaced as soon as possible. She turned back to the old droid, and wondered if want of a replacement system was what brought his life to an end.

'Just can't get the parts these days,' said a voice from the doorway behind her. Startled, she turned to see a man partially silhouetted by the bright daylight outside. As he entered the room she wondered why she had not heard him approach, as the sound of his spurs accompanied every footstep across the bare wooden floor.

'Is that why he died?' she asked. 'Something go wrong he couldn't replace?' The newcomer faced her.

'Near as I can tell without taking him apart. Came into my shop some time a few weeks back, muttering something about needing something. Looked all round my shelves for a while but left empty-handed, so guess he didn't find it, whatever it was.' He looked down at the still form in the armchair, then back at her. 'He your husband?'

The question took her by surprise. Not for what it asked, or for who asked it, but because she had no idea of the answer. Her confusion must have been evident, because the stranger spoke before she could reply.

'You know, I seen you in town a few times before—out and about. Usually he'd be with you, so I figured you two were involved in some way, be it husband and wife or family. What I also figure is that his passing had something of a contrary effect on you; not seen either one of you out in the town since he came to my shop. There a problem with your systems?'

This was one question to which she did know the answer. 'I ran a check, said my memory core regulator was in need of repair.' The stranger nodded as if this confirmed what he had been thinking.

'Them things are tricky gadgets, you won't find a new one out here. I'll take a look at it myself and see if it can be repaired if you'd like; owning the parts shop I have a few skills in that direction.'

'That would be most kind, sir,' she replied, 'but unless I recall wrongly, I have little enough to pay you with.' As she said this, the shopkeeper looked uncomfortable for the first time since he appeared.

'Well, ma'am, that was sort of the purpose of my visit. See, low as we are on parts around here, it's starting to get so that more and more droids are expiring for want of replacements. All the mines and plants hereabouts have shut down, so we've been asking folk if they mind us using core parts from their deceased. It's none too respectful, I'm aware, but times are real hard these days.'

'I understand,' she said. 'You may certainly use his parts to help any that need them.' It wasn't as if she could clearly remember the old droid anyway, and it seemed selfish to withhold help for no practical reason. An idea came to her as she considered this. 'Will you be able to replace my memory core regulator with his?' she asked.

'Well we can try ma'am, but I reckon he's been gone too long. Most core systems'll keep near indefinitely, but peripherals need the constant power flow or they corrode up beyond repair fast as you like.' He turned and with a deft motion lifted the old droid from the chair onto his back. 'If you'd care to follow me, we'll take this old droid to the shop and see if there's anything we can do for you.' He moved to the door and stepped out into the dry sun-beaten street. She followed him, blinking to shade her optical units against the sudden brightness.

Despite his burden, he set a brisk pace along the main street and she frequently had to run to keep up with him. It wasn't far to his shop, though; the town itself seemed small enough that everything was in close proximity to everything else. They soon arrived and the shopkeeper told her to wait just inside the doorway while he took the old droid into the back room, presumably for salvage. His voice carried through the open door to her:

'I used to have hired help doing the actual salvage and the like, but what with all these folk upping and leaving, I'm more or less on my own in here lately. Not that I really mind of course, always been one to keep to myself. You might want to see this, ma'am: come on through.' She did so, anxiety rising in her as she entered the well-lit back room. The walls were lined with tools and parts, but the floor was scrupulously tidy and there were four workbenches arranged in the centre. At the nearest stood the shopkeeper, his back to her. On the bench in front of him was the body of the old droid — her husband, apparently.

'What have you found?' she asked, almost dreading the reply though she couldn't think what it was that caused this apprehension. What could he have possibly seen that would upset her, or even be of much interest to her?

'This old droid didn't die for want of parts, ma'am. Everything's in working order — or it was when he died. I've seen this in a lot of the dead I've brought back here; he just gave up and shut himself down.'

✱

I don't recall everything as happened out in the wastes; the memories of the old towns are the clearest. But there's one thing I do remember true. A lot of bad things have been going on in recent times and I can trace them all back to where they began: that damned whore. All the proverbial workings came undone right at the very moment she screamed for help. But that's a good ways into my story, though the beginning itself is harder to place: I'll just start with what drove me to that whore's town.

All droids have a need for replacement parts. Old parts get worn out, or damaged, and when that happens your average droid'll head to the parts shop and get itself fixed. Me, I've been robbed of that luxury of late on account of this damned fool exodus back to the City, most droids abandoning their homes out in the wastes to go chase dreams. Maybe that's why they ventured out here in the first place, but way I see it both journeys are fool's errands. Whatever their reasoning, it means that the mines, workshops and parts stores are starting to fall down with no soul to tend them.

This spells quite the catastrophe for those such as I, though for all I know I'm alone in my ailment of needing near-constant replacement parts. Maker knows how this came about: damned if I can recall my own self why I am the way I am, but the fact is that there are no parts shops that can serve my needs. But fortune does occasionally smile on those in need, it seems, as this wave of discontent has kicked off not only the mass exodus back to the City, but also a rash of suicides in most every settlement you care to think of. I got nothing against others doing it, but you wouldn't catch me taking the easy way out; life's a fight and I'll be damned if I'm giving in that easy. One thing to be said in favour of suicide, though, is that it sure does provide an ample supply of replacement parts if you're fast enough.

The first corpse I cut open was a middle-aged female who kindly donated an optical processor. I don't full recall how I came across her, but I do remember how it felt to put the knife through her skin, revealing the circuitry and bare components beneath. It felt powerful, though it was clear it took little enough power to do it.

To the best of my knowledge, that first incident went unnoticed while I was in town. I stayed around for a few more days, haunting the back alleys and watching for any signs of suicides, preying upon the fresh corpses before the components had a chance to corrode, until I felt confident that I could get out of town with a fair chance of survival in the wastes before hitting the next settlement. I definitely had the impression that I should be moving on: there were rumours of what I'd been doing around town, and while the inflated stories of some dark menace lurking in the shadows provided me with no small degree of amusement, I figured it was time to be moving on.

So I set off into the wastes, pitted with abandoned mines and silent quarries, where the only souls you're like to see are those heading Citywards. I steered well clear of those Maker-forsaken convoys, drifting through the landscape like ghosts, everything about them screaming hopelessness and futility. Used their tracks to get me to wherever it was they came from, though, which in the first instance was a small one-time mining town up in some particularly inhospitable hills. Found only slim pickings there; for one reason or another the majority of droids had packed up and left town rather than ended their lives quickly and painlessly.

It wasn't a time to be picky though; I had parts that needed replacing, in particular my left motor periphery co-ordinator. Already I could feel my limbs on one side of my body responding sluggishly to commands, and it was only a matter of time before they packed it in altogether. Fortune smiled once more for me though, and I found a willing donor on the edge of town; seemingly he'd given up hope while staring out into the hills at the old mines, most like recalling finer days. Reckon if I'd found him a day later the parts I needed would have been useless.

My stay in that town was cut short by the untimely discovery of my victim, in spite of the fact I ditched him in a quarry pit. Some other lost soul must've wandered out for likely the same reasons as the first, my best guess. However it happened, it meant I had to get out of town in a hurry as there were a number of people looking for me with less than friendly intent. So I went out into the barren wastes again, and I'm guessing that death-hungry mob didn't dare follow me; ain't no need for a droid to venture out there unless he's running from something. That's why it's only me and the Citybound folk.

Memories of the wastes are most always hazy, one day blurs to another and the only thing as changes is my wretched shell wasting further away. This was the first time I got any close to perished out in the wastes, after being run out of that town. Few enough tracks around to show me the way to any other settlements nearby, so it took longer than I'd hoped, and I was in bad shape when a column of smoke on the horizon pointed me in the right direction.

Cresting a rise, I spotted my target: not the town I'd hoped for, but the wreckage of some poor bastard's ride. Drawing near, I figured it hadn't been long since the thing gave out on him, and he might well still be in the area. Luckily enough for me, the tracks were simple enough to follow, and took me a mile or so away to a hunched form on the top of the next hill. As I approached, I loosened my knife in its sheath; there was no time to lose, as I'd already lost all feeling in my right arm and sight in one optical unit.

The corpse was sat in the dirt, in the same position as when he had given up hope and switched off. Wasting no time, I knelt down behind him and pushed my knife into the back of the droid's skull to get to the optics components; a working right arm would do me no good if my other optical unit shut down first. Last thing I expected was the sharp bite of a power discharge to run down my blade, as it had never happened with any other corpse. Thought nothing of it at the time, though, and it was only after I'd taken a new optical unit and right peripheral motor control from the guy that I realised what the difference was between him and the dozen other corpses I'd cut up and salvaged.

This guy had been alive when I'd cut him open.

*

'Why would he do such a thing?' She didn't know where the note of alarm in her voice had come from; maybe it was feelings toward the old droid coming back to her, or just a general revulsion toward the thought of ending one's own life in the way that he had. Perhaps the shopkeeper had made a mistake, perhaps he hadn't killed himself after all, but had been let down by a core component that the shopkeeper had missed.

'I wouldn't know the why-for, ma'am, but it's unmistakable,' he replied, seeming to read her thoughts. 'Awful lot of droids these parts are doing the same, it seems; other folk are grabbing their gear and setting off for the City, they say. With both going on it's getting mighty quiet in town of late.'

'And nobody knows why this is happening?' she asked. It seemed inconceivable that this would all be happening without a good reason.

'Not so much that they'd talk about it, leastwise not with me; but there's a real feeling going around that this life is far too hard, so hard that folk're just giving right up. Those that do either pack up and leave, bound for the City, or they just shut themselves off. I'm sorry to tell you that your friend here numbers among the latter.'

She thought about this, and got a strange feeling as she did. 'You said that he was in your shop not long ago, looking over your shelves. If he had no need of a new part, why would he do that?'

The shopkeeper was clearly as confused as she was, but told her there was little more he could do. 'I've got what core components I could from him, so you can take him away for a proper burial if you want.'

She figured that would be the right thing to do, and with the shopkeeper's help she took him to the pits on the edge of town, where the town disposed of its dead. The shopkeeper handed over the old droid to the pit-tender and bid them both farewell. She thanked him for his troubles and watched as he turned and strode back to his shop.

The pit-tender was a hunched figure, the legacy of a life of digging pits and carrying corpses. He never seemed to make visual contact with her, which made her feel slightly uncomfortable in his presence.

'Another one offed himself, has he?' he asked cheerfully. 'Tell you they're dropping almost faster'n I can bury them these days. Always keep a few fresh pits ready and waiting, I do — never know when another stiff's going to show up.'

He set about his business with surprising speed, laying the old droid out in a pit and starting to shovel the dirt back over him. She was left standing by, watching and not quite knowing if she was supposed to be doing something. She decided to attempt conversation, as uncomfortable as she was with the pit-tender.

'Do you know why everyone's suddenly dying or leaving?' she asked, it being the question foremost in her mind at that moment. The pit-tender paused in his shovelling and gave her a half-glance, still not meeting her gaze. As he spoke, he resumed his task.

'It's the despair what's done it, I reckon. Folk find life out here too hard, scraping a living out of the rock and dirt. Start feeling useless they do, no point to their lives. Start giving up on it all, either kill theirselves or head back to the City 'cause they forgotten why they left in the first place.'

'What about those that stay?' she enquired. 'Why don't they leave with the rest, or end their lives?' She couldn't place her reason for such curiosity, except perhaps because of the old droid she was now watching being buried, and who had apparently been her husband.

'Can't speak for all of 'em, that's for sure. But as for myself, well you can plainly see I got myself a purpose here, grim as it is to other folk. Keeps the despair at bay, you might say. Sure I figure eventually town'll run outta customers for me, but until then I'm thinking I'll tick over just fine.' The pit-tender chortled to himself quietly. 'The droid from the parts shop, though, he got hisself a whole different reason for sticking around. Determined to help everyone, that droid; ever since I put his wife in the ground a fair old time back. After that, he started tending the parts shop and barely a day'd pass he wouldn't be out in the streets helping anyone he came across. Even dug me a few pits this one time when a whole family offed itself.' He patted the dirt flat and straightened as much as he could, bidding her good day as he shuffled off further into the pit-yard. She paused at the pit's edge, thinking about the old droid and wishing she could remember more about him.

With these thoughts in her head she turned and walked back through the dust-choked streets to the building that was apparently her home. It was just as bare and quiet as when she had left with the shopkeeper earlier. She decided to have a look around, though there were few enough rooms to investigate: just an upstairs bedroom and what appeared to be a workshop or study in the back. The walls in that room were lined with various tools — trowels, brushes, spades and knives hung next to shelves covered in strange pieces of metal and stone. On the workbench was a battered book entitled *Archaeology*, from one rudimentary printing press or another.

Flicking through, she found scribbled notes in the margins of the pages, giving opinions or dates and locations. They were in two differing hands, one of which she assumed was hers, the other her late husband's. One of the notes caught her attention, from the urgency with which it appeared to have been written:

Where is it?

It was in the margin next to a section headed 'Rumours and Conspiracy Theories'; the paragraph appeared to be about a vault in which there was some sort of relic from long ago, though the exact nature of it wasn't made clear. But with a sudden clarity, she knew that this was what the old droid — her husband — had been looking for in the parts shop: clues to find this vault. The more she looked around, the more she realised that this was what most of the items on the shelves were. Each was labelled with the time and place it was found, and what she presumed to be a page reference for the book. She sat on the basic stool in front of the workbench, and thought about all she had discovered. It appeared that the shopkeeper and the pit-tender weren't the only ones who had discovered a reason to stay.

❋

So it seemed I'd killed a droid for the first time, but speaking plain I didn't much care. Guy had given up on life and was most like going to sit there and expire anyhow: I just helped speed up the process and put parts to good use as would else have gone to waste. Best of it was that his central motor control fixed the problem with his bike, so I took his spurs and set off in the direction he had come from. It'd been a goodly long while since I'd last cruised along on one of those machines, and they were damned rare, but it felt good when I sank the spurs into the starter sockets and heard that first roar of the motor.

It took me far less time to get around in this fashion, so it wasn't long afore the town appeared in front of me. First thing that occurred was that it was far bigger than most I'd seen in my time, with a great many grand buildings. Second thing that occurred was that it'd be mighty tricky to track any one droid down in a place of such size, and that I might have finally found somewhere I could stay for a spell without no mobs or nothing nipping at my heels. I stashed the bike a way outside town, figuring some folk may recognise it and start asking less-than-welcome questions regarding its previous owner, and walked into town.

I had no true pressing need for any new parts as such, so I decided to set myself up with lodgings, as I was planning to stay a goodly while. With this in mind I wandered round the streets taking in what this town seemed to offer, though much of it was falling into disrepair. Of most interest, though, were two buildings sat next to each other: the larger was a brothel, full of droids both beautiful and expensive, and less so on each score. These places were a regular feature of towns across the wastes, but the size of this one was like nothing I'd witnessed with my own two optical units. The smaller building, however, was a truly strange sight; bars across the windows like it was a bank afraid of being robbed, but a bank it sure weren't. Sign above the door said 'LAW'.

Now I'd never really run into seriously organised rule-enforcement afore now, aside from one town which had what it called a Head Droid. Gave the guy a badge and a hat, he wandered around that small town as if he owned it, telling folk what to do and what not to do, generally making a real nuisance outta hisself. Eventually got to be so much of a thorn in everyone's side that they beat ten buckets of sense outta him and left him for dead. He didn't have an office of his own though, and something told me that the 'law' in this town could well be a force to be reckoned with. Figuring they had no way to know if I'd broken their rules yet or not, I crossed the street and entered the squat building.

It was none too bright in there, and the air had a distinctly unfriendly feel to it. There was a droid sat at a desk near the door who bore an uncanny resemblance to the building itself: he was short, squat and had LAW writ large on his black shirt. Beyond him was a short corridor bordered by cages on either side, a few of which were occupied. The droid in the black shirt looked up at me as I walked in, and his gaze continued his seeming similarity with the building: there was little in the way of welcome to be found. But I've never been one to be put off by a simple lack of welcome, and told him I was new in town and needed to know what rules they had so as I didn't go breaking any without knowing.

'New in town?' said he. 'Yeah, you'll be wanting to stay on the right side of the law here. Whyfore'd you leave your last town?'

Told him I'd been wandering the wastes long as I could remember, never really had a true home but thought I'd try my hand at it in this place 'til such a time as I tire of the life or such. He seemed suspicious, but something told me he always did. He dug his hand into a drawer of the desk and pulled out a slender book which he pushed across the surface toward me; unsurprisingly, the single word on the cover was 'LAW'. I took the book and thanked him for his time, getting little more than a cursory grunt in way of a reply.

Back in the street I continued my leisurely journey through the town, flicking through the book as I went. Seems most things were frowned upon by the law-men in these parts, but I was most interested to find there was nothing stated about them having a problem with the cutting up of corpses. Guess if they had a rule against it the parts shops and the like would go out of business pretty quick — what with all the fleeing droids and suicides, a whole load of them are starting to salvage from corpses. Industry itself seems a fair corpse at this point.

Being a creature of habit, I wasn't like to change my ways just on account of some droids with badges who were too big for their boots and lived for bossing people around. So I found myself an abandoned home as they were sure easy enough to come by, and set myself up in this little hideaway. The first night came down fast, and it wasn't long afore the street was black and empty, save for a few pools of light around hanging lamps. I set out on my first night of business, with a shopping list from my self-diagnostics.

As I'd not been around this town too much, I stuck to the fringes so as to stay clear of most of the people. Thought it was a real stroke of luck when I happened upon an old storage shed, half a mile out of

town, with a faint light spilling out from between the boards. There
was nothing else even close by, but I crept up nice and quiet just to
be sure. From the size of the thing I figured it couldn't easily hold
more than two droids at once, and as I got in close I heard sounds
that told me that were exactly what it was holding. I considered
heading back to town and finding a droid on its own somewhere,
an easy mark; but there was no chance I'd find a spot this quiet, so
I figured I'd try my luck.

I moved silently to the back of the building and peered through a
gap in the boards. He had her against one of the side walls, and her
head was turned toward the back wall. They both had their optical
shades closed, and were making enough noise to cover anything I
might have done, so I slipped round to the front and very quietly
opened the door. They made no sign to show they'd seen or heard
me, and I silently took up a pick axe from against the far wall.

The doorway provided just enough room to swing it, and its
point sunk heavily into the bottom of the guy's back, a spot which
my previous activities had told me would irreparably damage his
lower motor functions and stop the bastard running for good. He
stiffened and fell back, lodging the pick firmly where it had hit; the
girl stared and then started to scream. I didn't know if it was loud
enough to reach folk in town, but that wasn't a chance I was about
to take. The pick was unusable now, but I grabbed a sledgehammer
and swung it at the bitch; first time she dodged well enough and it
went through the wall, but on the second try I struck her clean in
the head and it was that as went through the wall. Never did find
it myself, but I figure it was beyond salvage anyhow.

I worked quickly, taking components I needed from the guy's
head and the girl's body, then split. Hared it back to my room and
waited for the morning; thought as I ran that I saw a light moving around on the edge of town, though what it was I didn't stick
around to find out.

Morning came bright and clear as it always did, and I decided to
head for the saloon to calm down from the night's activities. It was
on the way there that I noticed something that changed my thinking on this town's law-men: nailed to many a wall down the street
was a notice headed with the word 'MURDER!'. Reading down the

page it became clear that not only were the law-men here powerful and determined, but they also had the respect of the people. On top of this, the poster made clear that one of their nightly patrols had glimpsed a shadowy figure fleeing the area of the crime. All these facts together were going to spell trouble for me, I knew. Looking back, I should have got out of there right at that moment; but I figured I'd be fine, long as I was careful. Not sure as I've ever been more wrong.

She wasn't sure of much at that moment, but she knew a few things that were enough: she was an archaeologist, as her husband had been; they had been searching for some sort of vault; this vault was of incredible importance; and she would continue the search for as long as it took. She had found an old backpack with a tent in it under the desk, and had loaded as many relics as she could into it along with the tools. Many of the relics were rather weighty, so she had to choose which would be the most useful and pack those; she also packed one which had never been identified: a large piece of metal, a strangely-shaped rod. While she had no real idea where she was bound, the book and notes provided just enough to go on for the time being.

Her first stop was a gully a few miles outside the town. The notes in the book told her that was where most of the first finds had been made, and pointed to some sort of large gathering or settlement. It seemed to take days to walk that far, though in reality it could not have been more than a few hours; though when she finally arrived it was starting to get dark. She set up her tent and slept the night away, dreaming strange dreams of the old droid beckoning her to enter a vault: when she tried to follow, it was nothing but a rock face before her.

She awoke with the morning sun cutting through the thin fabric of her tent, and wasted no time in getting to work. The gully wasn't long or deep, but unusually wide; the notes told her that it was at the widest point that the majority of finds had been unearthed, and so that was where she began to dig. She wasn't at all certain of what she might discover, but hoped it would give her some idea of where to go next,of where the vault was. She dug countless pits in the gully bed, but nothing even remotely useful came to light, and as the day wore on she despaired of ever finding anything.

As the sun set once more, she retired back to her tent to sleep, but for a long while lay awake, unable to stop thinking about the vault. Why was it she had found absolutely nothing in all the pits she had dug? Surely she hadn't come to the wrong place? No, the notes were very specific about where to go, this had to be the right place; but it was so hard to believe that so many finds had come from this barren gully. Then it hit her: perhaps she had found nothing because there was nothing left. Perhaps the gully had been picked clean of even the smallest item. The relief this brought was soon replaced by fresh despair: if there was nothing left to find, then all she had to go on was what had already been found and recorded by herself and her husband.

She sat, and lit the lamp next to her, pulling out the book and most of the relics. There was a battered tin lantern, very much like her own, which had been one of the first things found at the site. Turning to the back of the book, she sketched a rough plan of the gully, plotted the point at which the lantern had been found. She then proceeded to do the same for every item she had with her, and the picture it painted for her slowly took shape.

There had been a camp of some sort here, a long time ago. The tent pegs told her that it was a temporary camp rather than a permanent settlement, but there were also some planks and boards that suggested there was one slightly more substantial building in the centre. What purpose it all served, however, still eluded her, and provided no clues as to the vault's whereabouts. She sighed, and the thrill of discovery she had felt started to fade as she realised she had gained little or nothing from this exercise. She sighed, and laid herself back down to sleep, reaching over to switch off the lamp.

As she did so, however, one of the relics caught her gaze. It was a piece of board from the central building, and at first she wasn't sure why it had suddenly attracted her attention; then she thought she saw something scratched into the surface. The more she looked, the more it looked like shapes — no, letters — had been carved into the wood. Trying to make them out, she could only piece together a few words: follow, failed, change, north, mine. They made no real sense on their own but she realised that when taken in the context of the vault it became quite clear. Whoever had made this camp was attempting to build the vault; something went wrong, and the plans were changed. They went north, looking for a mine — or, she supposed, heading towards a specific mine; it didn't matter which. She made a note in the book about this new revelation, and settled down to get some sleep. She had a long walk ahead of her in the morning.

Again the sunlight awoke her as it streamed into the tent, and swiftly she packed everything away into the backpack, setting off into the wastes. There were no more clues in the relics she already had, nor in what notes she and her husband had made; they had evidently not travelled out much farther than the gully. She would have to hope beyond hope that there would be something in this mine — perhaps even the vault itself. But what was she even expecting that to be?

Days passed, though the monotony of travelling through the wastes meant that she found it hard to count them. Eventually though, she caught a shine on the horizon; the sun was reflecting from something in the hills ahead of her. As she drew near, she saw that it was a small settlement approximately the same size as her own. The thrill of discovery again coursed through her as she noticed that in the hills were the unmistakable black spots that signified the presence of a mine.

Looking back later, she could never recall walking through the town; it was as if she had no sooner seen the mine than was entering a minor side tunnel. What sent her into that particular shaft she didn't know, but it didn't take her long to find something by the light of her lantern. At first it seemed just to be an incomplete tunnel, ending as it did in a flat wall of rock; on closer inspection, however, she saw that it was blackened — the result of a fire. There were no other clues, however; just a few rocks and planks. She decided it was probably too dangerous to dig up the tunnels, and headed back towards daylight to gather her thoughts.

On the way back, she tripped over something she hadn't really noticed on the way in. It was quite large, and seemed at first to be a rounded rock. She picked it up to examine, and found that it was charred at one end. It wasn't until she put it down that she realised what it was — it made a strange sound as if it were made of metal. Kneeling down and peering closer, she thought she could make out certain indentations in its surface; as she looked at it, her mind started forming a familiar pattern from these shapes and indentations.

It was a face.

✱

After seeing that poster I was in more need of a strong drink than I had been to start with, so I headed to the saloon and sat down at the bar. I wasn't far surprised that the barkeep was still in business — with all the despair spreading around, saloons must have been doing a roaring trade. At that time of day though, I was the only one in there. Barkeep came over and nodded to me, taking in my dusty coat and clothes as he did.

'Bit early for drinking, ain't it?' said he. 'Not that I'd turn away the custom, mind, just ain't used to having company 'til sun's well up.' I answered that it'd been a long night, and that seemed to do the trick. Guess you don't get to be a barkeep long without knowing when to stop asking questions. He poured me a drink.

'Hear it was a shorter night for some,' he continued in a conversational tone. 'Young couple on edge of town were going at it in a tool shed, some madman interrupts their fun — with deadly force, as you might say.'

'You don't say,' said I. 'That happen often in this town?'

'Maker, no!' he replied, the truth of his words plain on his face. 'Not been a droid killed another for years — not since we got the law-men to keep the peace.'

'Must do a damned good job of it, from what I seen.'

'Best as they can, I reckon.' He leant across the bar and his voice became bare more than a whisper. 'You know, those droids last night weren't just killed. I hear tell their bodies were cut on, and bits of their workings taken. Ain't right that, you know. Not right at all.'

'Law-men got any leads?' I asked, truly curious for my own sake.

'Naw. 'Bout all they got is the word of one of their patrols who saw someone running from the scene, but nothing close to a suspect.'

I paid and thanked him for the drink and the chat, then left the bar. Seemed to me that I couldn't afford another near-miss like that, or it might not be a miss at all next time. I'd underestimated the law-men here; they were far more organised than I was expecting. Still, the town was big and I figured as long as I was careful and kept my head down I should be able to stick around a while longer, which meant finding an excuse to do so.

With that in mind, I headed across to the pit-yard, and found it untended. After asking around the area for a while, I discovered that the previous pit-tender had switched off after finding his wife had done the same. Nobody was around to bury the dead at that time, so it seemed I'd found myself a job. It was easy enough work, digging holes and filling them with a stiff. Every so often I'd be brought a fresh corpse and made sure I cut them up good and took what I needed before putting them in the ground.

Things continued on in this fashion for quite some time, and only occasionally did I get to the point of having to sneak into somebody's house in the dead of night to get me some salvage. Still, every time I did the law-men put up another poster; eventually there were some as stayed up the whole time. These were headed 'WANTED', and detailed my crimes against the town; nothing about that worried me though, they had no description to go on. The rumours started spreading about a serial killer on the loose, and some even called this shadowy figure 'the Reaver'. I do believe that I may enter the folklore of that place, and become some mythical threat that droids scare each other with: if there are any droids left to tell the stories, that is.

I started to get uneasy about things before too long though. It all happened back in the saloon, where I spent many an evening after working in the pit-yard all day. I was sat in my accustomed spot at the bar when a conversation drifted into my hearing from a table not far behind me.

'How come you didn't get hauled off for smacking that whore?' asked one.

'Law-man must'a seen she were in the wrong. Paid good money for her, she refused to service me on account o' my wife being a friend o' hers. Stupid whore don't know her place.'

''Course,' put in a third droid 'could be as they just got their hands full lookin' fer the Reaver. Heard he took another two nights back, cut his gut open while he was still alive.' This was true enough; the guy had been beating his wife earlier that day and I wasn't about to be polite with what I went there to do.

'Ah, quit with yer stories, would ya?' begged the fourth. 'Always tryin' to put the scares on folk.'

'Well I fer one ain't afraid of no killer!' the whore-beater said.

'Maybe you should be,' said the one who seemed to like scaring folk. 'They say those as ain't afraid are the ones running fastest when the Reaver comes for 'em.'

'Quit callin' him that!' the fourth said. 'Ain't no Reaver, just a droid gone loco.' A quiet fell over the table, and I felt rather than saw the glances in my direction. The conversation continued in hushed tones.

'Guy at the bar's a new boy in town, y'know. Came in not long back. Anyone else notice the killings started about when he showed up?'

'Reckon you're right. Could be as he's this killer the law-men are out for.'

'Would you stop with your damned stories for one minute?' shouted the fourth, punctuating his demand by throwing his fist into the face of the droid telling all the stories. Through some unspoken agreements the four droids paired up and began beating each other senseless. Shortly, a figure I later identified as the whore-beater flew past my head, still accelerating as he smashed into the bottles behind the bar. The situation rapidly broke down into an all-out bar brawl, and I managed to get out the door before getting caught up in the violence. Seemed as the issue of my possible identity was also lost in the fight, but it sure as hell got me more than a little apprehensive.

✽

After finding the droid's head, the archaeologist had stayed in the mine another two days, digging and excavating wherever she thought it was safe to do so. Though finds were few and far between, she did begin to build up a picture of what the place had been. It seemed that this tunnel had been intended as the entranceway to the vault, but as it was being excavated there had been some sort of accident (accounting for the burning, and indeed the head) which resulted in the project being abandoned and moved elsewhere. Most excitingly, however, she also gained some insight into what the exact nature of the vault might be: from what she could piece together, it seemed to be some sort of bunker, but on a far grander scale.

What she couldn't seem to find, however, was anything to tell her where the builders of the vault had relocated to after this second failure in their mission. So after two days in the mine, she walked back down to the town to try her luck there.

The locals were friendly enough, but it quickly became clear that they knew nothing of the vault or the mission into the nearby mine; everyone she asked professed ignorance or just looked at her strangely and hurried away. Even presenting the head had gained no response better than ridicule or revulsion. What could she do now? It appeared that her journey had reached an impasse, and while she was certain the builders had moved on, she had no idea where they may have moved to. As she sat on a bench in the street to think about this, she took out the book to go back over her notes and perhaps spot some pattern she had previously not seen. It was hopeless, though; even what she had already written started making little enough sense to her.

But then a thought occurred to her: what of the author of the book himself? Wouldn't he know where to look, or at least what to look for? But where to look for him? She showed the book to passers-by, and eventually one of them mentioned that the next town had a printing press that may well have been the one to print that volume. Most fortunate of all, however, was that there was a group of droids moving to that town, setting off that same day, so she didn't have to face weeks of trackless wastes on her own. Thanking the droid who had helped her, she ran to meet the caravan.

It took them six days to reach their destination, and no sooner had they arrived than she set off asking directions to the printing press. It didn't take long to find, though it was far smaller than many of the buildings in the centre of town. Entering, she was greeted by a friendly young droid who appeared to be the only one working there.

'Sure, I remember that old book,' he replied when she showed it to him and asked about it. 'It was a fair time back, but I don't print many books around here these days and I remember fondly the ones I used to. Recently all I've been printing is bad news, "Wanted" posters and the like.'

'Do you happen to know if the author is still around?' she asked.

'Why, of course, the old guy lives right across the street from here. Still comes in every few days: think he just likes the feel of the place, y'know?'

She thanked him for his help and went to the building the young droid had pointed out to her. It was a long while before the door was answered, and she started to despair of finding anyone at home. When the door finally opened, it was to a miserable-looking weather-beaten face, which glared at her until she asked if he were the author she was looking for.

'Yeah, I'm the one as wrote that book,' he replied 'though it was longer ago than I care to remember. What of it?' He stared impassively while she recounted her story.

'You're looking for the vault?' he asked when she had finished. She nodded. 'You realise it don't exist, right? That's why it's in the section of my book entitled "Conspiracies and Rumours" or some-such. I only threw it in on account o' I had a few pages left to fill as I was paying for anyhow. Now if you're quite done wasting every-body's time, I'll bid you good day.'

The door was slammed in her face, and she stood for a number of minutes trying to process what she'd just heard. It had to exist, surely. What about all the things she'd found?

She turned and walked to the saloon she had noticed on her way into town, its windows and furniture smashed as if there had been a brawl there recently. It was late in the day, so there were a few people in there, but not as many as there would be once the sun set. She didn't drink as such, but had heard it described as a cure for one's problems, so ordered one. Not long after she sat down at a quiet table near the door, another droid walked in, and after a glance around the room, he came across to her.

'I overheard your conversation with that crotchety old man back there,' he said. 'Now, it's no business of mine, but I thought I ought to tell you what I know anyhow.' Hope surged high in her chest and she asked him to continue. 'Well, the vault he wrote about might be fictional as he claims, or it may not — either way, he sure as hell didn't make it up hisself. It's a part of local folklore which tells of these droids as came here when this town was barely more'n a saloon and a few shacks. None left from those days, so no-one knows what happened first-hand. Anyway, these droids went up into the hills, and the story goes that they were never seen again on account o' they dug a huge vault into the hill, bigger'n any mine. Filled it with everything they needed, and more besides — made it a real paradise in there. Then the entrance was lost or shut for good, and no droid's been able to find it since. But then, most these days don't look at all, figuring it's just a myth. Maybe they're right, but that shouldn't stop you looking.'

She couldn't believe her luck. Only moments ago she had despaired of ever finding the vault, even doubting its existence; now she found she was only a short way from the very thing she had travelled so far to find. Thanking the droid profusely for his help, and leaving him enough money to drink all night if he wished, she left the saloon. The light was starting to fade, but she had her lantern, and she didn't want to waste a moment when she could be discovering the vault itself. She headed into the hills.

✱

For the next couple of days after the brawl in the saloon, I kept a low profile, hoping that the corpses brought to the pit-yard would be enough to sustain me for a while. It seemed, though, that whatever luck I had enjoyed previously was starting to walk out on me, as a whole bunch of systems started degrading at once. Got so bad I was forced back into town in daylight: a risky gamble but it seemed to be a choice between take the risk or perish there and then. I wasn't ready to give up on life just yet, so I made my way through the streets, being careful as I could not to attract undue attention.

Most of the houses on the edge of town were unoccupied these days it seemed, and I ended up in the back alleys in the area of the main street. Looking through the windows as I went along, I saw that even most of the buildings along here were empty. I eventually found one as wasn't though: could see through to the front room of the house, where the old droid as lived there was talking to some-one at outside. Took the opportunity to climb in quietly through the window and wait for him to conclude his business. Couldn't hear what was being discussed, but it wasn't long afore I heard the door slam and the old droid come back through toward me, muttering under his breath. I took my knife out of its sheath at my side.

As he entered the room I threw the knife hard as I could at his temple, knowing that was one of the few spots as would shut him down swift. I'd done that move plenty of times before, and it had always worked a treat; this time, though, my co-ordination was off and it just took off the guy's nose. The knife clattered to the floor near the far wall, and the droid yelled in surprise, turning to face me. I wasted no time and launched myself at him, sending us both sprawling across the floor. I snatched up my knife again and turned to where he lay on his back. As he attempted to rise, I laid my knee on his chest and leant on him with all my weight, pinning him down.

He kept thrashing around making it so as I couldn't drive my knife anywhere as might finish him off easy, so I used it to saw through his neck instead, sending oil spurting across the wooden floor. He stopped screaming when I got about half way through, and I took what I could from him. Lot of his systems were in bad shape though, and I still needed a couple of replacements. Just had to hope that nobody had heard him screaming. I climbed back out the window and walked around to the front of the building, out into the street. There was no commotion, so I figured no-one had heard the old droid die. I crossed the street to the nearest building and slipped inside quietly.

It was dark inside, and there wasn't much in the way of floor space. Big machines took up most of the room, and were making enough noise to cover any that I might make. I couldn't even tell if I was alone in there or not though, and it was only when I turned the corner and came face to face with a young droid that I realised I did indeed have company. He looked confused, then alarmed; he must have seen the knife I held ready in my hand. My reflexes were not what they should have been: he got the first hit in, sending me reeling to the wall behind. He hesitated, clearly not sure whether to run or fight. I wasn't about to waste that opportunity: I ran at him ready to strike. He raised a hand to fend me off, but I changed the angle of my thrust to slice through his wrist, severing the motor lines and rendering his right hand useless.

He fell back, cradling his injured hand, and I struck him across the face with the hilt of my knife, turning him half around. As I did so, though, the knife fell from my grip and clattered to the floor underneath one of the machines. I grabbed him from behind, and kept a hold of him, both hands on his head. Turning him slightly, I smashed his head onto the edge of the nearest machine, time and time again. Still he struggled, but still I kept forcing him down. Eventually it must have damaged an important system: he stopped struggling. I let him go and he staggered about the room in a daze, crashing into everything as he went. To be honest I was surprised to see him still alive, but I soon changed that; I hefted a long heavy piece of metal and brought it down square on the top of his head. The last surge of power shot up the metal and I felt it rush into me, quickly fading.

I used the piece of metal to retrieve me back my knife and set about taking the young fella's parts. At least the bastard hadn't screamed when he died. I figured the law-men'd take a while to find him; long enough in any case to get me gone. Thankfully this droid's parts were in good nick, and I didn't need any more to keep me going, so I left the corpse and the building behind me.

In an idea that seemed good at the time, I thought I'd relax after my afternoon's exertions. The sun had just set, and I'd heard tell the girls in the brothel could take a man's mind off anything in the world, though that must be a tall order in these days of suicide and despair. Figured it couldn't hurt though, so I went over there and got me a room with a very friendly girl who I could tell was far more bright than they made her act for her clients. Wasn't exactly her smarts as I was interested in though, and she sure had curves aplenty for my tastes, and a customised manipulation device attached to her right hand which I was itching to test out. As I followed her up the stairs, she lifted her skirt, giving me a full view of her dynamos.

I threw my coat on the hook on the back of the door, and laid down on the bed. She climbed on top of me and started to unbutton my shirt; I stopped her and told her to go first. I felt the stirrings of arousal as she took off the red and black corset that had been barely containing her. The next thing I felt was distinctly less pleasant: a sharp stabbing sensation in my chest that sent waves of pain through my whole body. I'd had this once before; the diagnostic alarm told me it was the power flow unit in the centre of my chest, and there was never any warning for it giving out like this. I needed a replacement right there and then or I'd perish within the minute; as much as she'd please me, the whore had to be the one to donate me a new unit.

I reached for the knife at my belt and as I brought it out another spasm of pain hit me, throwing my arms out and sending the knife flying from my hand. The whore stared in shock at me, then at the knife on the floor by the window, quickly putting the facts together.

'It's you!' she cried. 'You're that damned Reaver, ain't you? Well, you ain't takin' me, that's fer sure!' She leapt off the bed and, still half-naked, went for the door, screaming for help. I quickly rolled off the bed, grabbed the knife, stood, and threw. It landed true, and she fell to the floor before she could get any further. There was no hope that her screams had gone unnoticed, and I had to work quickly through the pain to get her power flow unit out of her chest. I felt faint as I removed my own, but soon recovered with her healthy unit in me.

I quickly considered escape strategies, but my options were severely limited by the droids smashing through the door to investigate the ruckus. It didn't take them too long to work out what was going on and who I was, but by the time they started for me I was jumping out of the window.

✻

Her CPU was in overdrive as she climbed up the slope at the back of town. She was finally here, after all this time searching for the vault; she'd actually found it. So excited was she, in fact, that she very nearly ran straight past the tunnel, hidden as it was behind a large boulder. 'But that would make sense, wouldn't it?' she thought to herself. 'The builders seem to have wanted privacy from the world.'

Easing herself past the boulder, she entered the tunnel. It was black as a pit in there so she lit her lantern, casting a pool of light into the darkness. The tunnel was rough and unmarked, suggesting it was actually a natural cave. With every step, though, she found evidence that she was on the right path — arrows carved into the wall pointing her on, lamps hanging from the walls, long starved of fuel. She even started to see footprints on the floor of the tunnel, which must have been preserved there for time unknown.

Finally, she came up against a flat surface, much like the one she had found in the first mine all those days ago. This one, however, was not marked by burning, and she could see markings all over it, even the glow of power and the paths of circuitry beneath the surface. There was no doubt in her mind: this was the door of the vault. She had finally arrived. All she had to do was open it.

She searched the surface for handles, or buttons, but found none. She started to think there was no way to open it — why would there need to be, if the builders' intention was to simply live in there forever away from the world? But no, something about that didn't make sense. There had to be a way to open the door. Her mind threw something at her — a relic. That was it. There was a relic that had never been identified, found at that first site in the gully outside her old town. She dug into her backpack and when she couldn't find it, upended the bag, scattering the relics across the floor of the tunnel. On her hands and knees she searched through the finds, eventually locating the large piece of metal she was looking for.

Examining the door again, she found a hole, the same sort of shape as the piece of metal. Inserting the relic, she heard a click and a grinding noise, as if a lock was being withdrawn. Gingerly, she pushed on the door. It swung wide open, revealing a brightly-lit corridor and, beyond, a city.

She could scarcely believe her optical units. After everything she had been through, she was finally here, and it was more beautiful than she had ever imagined. She stood and just gazed at it, mesmerised by the sight, and started to laugh. Finally, she was at her journey's end.

✴

Turns out that folk didn't take none too kindly to murderers and whatnot in that town. This mob didn't look likely to stop any time soon as they ran after me, and something told me that they weren't looking to hand me over to the law-men so as I could go sit in a cell for a while. They meant to visit my misdeeds back on me, and I wasn't liking that prospect too well.

As I ran I thought of where I could go, but nowhere in town was safe. Out of town then, to where I'd stashed the bike. As soon as I was on that I'd be long gone and the town naught but a bad memory fading behind me: but that was on the other side of town, in the opposite direction to where I was heading. I turned and hared down an alleyway between two shops, leaping over boxes and bins as I went. I could still hear the mob on my heels, and every alley I passed leading onto the main street showed me glimpses of my pursuers. They were growing in numbers, that was for sure.

Eventually I got to the edge of town and ran out into the wastes, hoping I could remember where I'd stowed the thing. The lights of lanterns had just started to clear the last buildings behind me when I reached the right place; I remember I'd put it there because the shape of the gully was very distinctive, like a sickle. The bike, however, was gone. Now I'm certain there was something in that damned rule book of theirs about not stealing, and I laughed bitterly as I realised I was cursing those as wanted to catch me for not doing their job right. I thought quickly; where else could I go? Had to be somewhere they wouldn't follow.

I should probably have headed out into the wastes, but I remembered how isolated this town was, and didn't like my chances of making it to another town before something or other vital gave out on me. Frankly, my hopes of survival were better in the hands of the mob. I looked around, and remembered the hills outside town; it had to be easier to hide there than out here where the ground was flatter than a blade. I set off towards them, making sure I steered well clear of the path of the townsfolk.

It struck me as I ran that I couldn't quite recall why they were chasing me; a self-diagnostic showed my memory core regulator was malfunctioning. Great; one more thing to go wrong. I fought against the memory loss as I ran, constantly reminding myself who I was, why I was running, and what I had to do: hope beyond hope that I could find someone on their own out here who would donate their regulator. I tried not to think about how hideously unlikely that was, and concentrated on running up the slopes of the hill as fast as I could, looking out for hiding places as I went.

I thought maybe my luck had changed when I found the entrance to a tunnel obscured behind a large boulder, and I quickly dived inside hoping nobody following had seen me. I'd found somewhere to hide, but without a regulator I'd quickly forget why I was here and wander on outside. I kept going through the darkness, and it seemed to me that it was getting brighter as I went; I could make out details around me. The floor was totally smooth except for one set of footprints heading deeper into the tunnel. There was a strange sound, too: almost like somebody laughing. Eerier than I liked, that.

I turned a corner and saw the answer to all my questions: there was a female droid standing in front of a blank wall, lantern at her feet and arms thrown wide. There was a bag on the floor surrounded by lots of rocks with labels on them. Maker knows why she was laughing, but I wasn't about to ask her. My knife slid easily into the back of her head and her laughter stopped. I quickly replaced my memory core regulator with hers, and waited to notice a change.

I walked out of the tunnel, and saw a crowd there to greet me. They seemed angry for some reason, but before I could ask why, the first blow landed to my head. I remember nothing more.

Cayuse

Colleen Weare

'By the Maker's rusty cogs! It ain't so bad around here that things can't get worse!'

Josie removed her hat as she surveyed the smoking ruins of the homestead, sunlight glittering off the sculpted blued gunsteel covering her skull. Temporarily deprived of shade, her optical receptors had to quickly adjust to the harsh glare of the noonday sun. Slapping the dust from her hat, she plopped it back on her head.

Wreckers and renegades. Her horse Paint communicated via their wireless connection, lowering his head to sniff at the charred wreckage of the house. Cautiously he stepped over the rubble of the outer wall formed of stone and timber. It had been caved in by some powerful force, the mortar anchoring stone and old lumber had shattered like glass under the assault. *Looks like they had at least two, maybe three heavy owlhoots with them. People didn't stand a chance.*

'They put up a good fight, though,' said Josie, speaking her thoughts aloud as well as through the comm-link they shared. Rising in the stirrups, she used that small height advantage to survey the area. 'Wreckers have vamoosed; they're probably halfway to the Iron Hills by now.' All the same, she kept her hands by the grips of her pistols, fingers relaxed and ready to respond at a moment's notice.

As she scanned the sere landscape beyond the home, her horse tracked through the smouldering remains of the ranch house, pushing aside chunks of burned beams with his metallic fore-hooves and poking his nose around in the still warm ashes. Satisfied for the moment that no more outlaws lurked in the scrubby hills surrounding them, Josie looked down over Paint's multicoloured neck. 'Any survivors?'

Haven't found any. The equine lifted his head, ears pointed sharply forward. *The IR signature's all washed out from the embers, no help for finding people.* He stepped sideways, turning his head. *Wait a moment!* Springing into the air, causing Josie to give an outraged yelp and grab at the saddle horn, he cleared a broken down wall and landed in what was once the farmhouse common room. The floor sounded hollow under his hooves, and he began to dig vigorously through the rubble and the ashes. Soon he had exposed a large area of planked floor.

'Hello down there! Hold on, we'll have you out in a moment!' Josie sprang from the saddle and ran her hands around the edges of the trapdoor Paint had found, searching for the catches. Before she could locate them, the door clicked and pushed up a fraction, enabling her to grasp the edges and lift it. Terrified faces peered into the bright daylight: a group of men clutching old rifles, a few women, and one child. Josie smiled at them. 'It's alright folks, the outlaws have gone. It's safe to come out.'

One by one, she helped the droids out of their hiding place. Exclamations peppered the dusty air as the people began to discover the extent of the damage.

'Maker preserve us!'

'Where'd the barn go?'

'Everything's burned up, Father, and the smelter's wrecked!'

'All the ingots have been stolen, too.'

'What a mess!'

'Who're you?' This last question was directed at Josie by one of the younger women, as she tried in vain to dust the dark charcoal smudges from her skirt.

'I'm Josie, sheriff of Cayuse. Sheriff Bill retired last year. I'd been his deputy for about ten years, so I took over after he left.' She pointed toward the rugged ochre hills to the west. 'I was riding this way after me an' the other law-folk put down a gang of hijackers on the other side of Coaltown.' Josie shifted in place. A stray ray of sunlight penetrated the smoky haze and glinted off the star pinned to her shirt. 'You were smart to have this hiding spot prepared, very smart.'

'Smart!' The speaker, an older female droid, shook her head, her shoulders slumped in defeat. 'This is the third time in so many years. We've had enough. It ain't smart anymore, just habit.'

'I know it's hard, the rebuilding and all, but Cayuse isn't that far away, the townsfolk will help — if memory serves me, your family has been mining and finding high-grade ores around here for years. If you want, we can get you set up in a new homestead and mining stake closer in toward Cayuse or Coaltown, where those of us who keep the law will be able to protect you. The mines in these parts attract outlaws, sorry to say.' Josie's smile turned sad. 'There just aren't enough of us to cover all this territory like it needs. Paint's fast, but he can't gallop at light speed.'

One of the men shook his head, started to speak and coughed dryly. Josie quickly pulled her canteen from the saddle and offered it to him. He took a long drink of the coolant inside, sighed deeply, and said. 'I'm Virgil, head of what was Red Ore Mine. I've heard of you, Sheriff. My wife Ella is right, we've had enough. We've worked the mines and homesteaded out here for over fifty years. Every time we make the least little gain, it gets taken away by thieves, grifters, and wreckers. It was the same in Leadville and in Yellowfork before that. We've rebuilt our homestead an' our bodies so many times I've lost count. We're tired of starting over.' Raising his head, he looked at the assembled adults, silently collecting their assent to an unspoken question. 'We'll follow you to any town you pick, Sheriff Josie. As soon as we can find transport and get packed up, we'll be leaving for the City.'

The City. The word dropped into Josie's mind like a heavy chunk of raw iron falling down a dark mine shaft, soundless but weighty as it plunged into the depths. Josie put Ella, the elderly lady, up on Paint's back. In front of Ella she put the child. Once the rest of the family had finished collecting what few items had survived the blaze, she walked out through the rubble and up the farm path toward the dusty track that led toward Cayuse. Paint followed her lead, his head at her shoulder. Behind the spotted horse trailed the family, walking patiently in the warm dust stirred up by their feet.

The landscape around them was harsh and utterly dry, edged with jagged mountains which hid rich deposits of metal ores and coal. The land topside was utterly arid, with the occasional breath of hot, dusty wind. Mining had drawn a population of droids to this area of the world. Towns had grown up around the sprawling mines and small stakes, their residents gleaning support from the ore. The towns turned out products the population needed for life and functionality: conductive wire, metals and ceramics for expanding and enhancing one's physical body, and components of all sorts.

Unfortunately, the bounty of metals, electronics, and other products the droids found necessary also attracted those droids who chose to prey on others rather than eke out an honest living. With the rise of thieves, bushwhackers, and wreckers came the need for protection, and so the towns had over the years selected those bold few who would take on the lawless. Lawmen who survived the initial learning process trained their successors, handing on their badges when time and wear — both mental and physical — caused them to retire. The slow evolution had been haphazard, each town developing its own system of laws and retaining those who kept them. The laws and codes were admittedly rudimentary, but in this land of the lawless, rough justice sufficed for most people. Josie was among the latest in a cadre of Cayuse sheriffs and deputies who had managed to endure years of adventure and hardship. Thoughts of defeat were alien to her nature, and mention of the City sounded like surrender.

'The City. I've heard of it,' she said flatly. 'Why return now?'

'You weren't made there, were you, child?' The once shiny metal covering Ella's face and hands showed the ravages of time and the harsh environment. Obviously the family had not had time or money perhaps to spend on cosmetic repairs to their older adult members. The child's outer shell was in much better repair, but like most newly made children, she was small and had been cobbled together from salvage and hand me downs. She had been made with loving care, however, with a finely crafted face. Masses of shining copper filaments made from ore drawn from the family mine framed her face and expressive blue optics. Her dress was clean and well kept, if somewhat patched and besmirched with soot from the fire. She sat the horse in front of her mother or grandmother, watching and listening intently.

'No, I'm third-generation Cayuse made,' said Josie. 'I've only heard stories of the City from the old-timers, and even they hadn't actually come from there. I'm not convinced it's a real place.'

'Oh, it's real all right. It's the City of the Maker, the place from which all of us came, by one way or another.' Ella's face lit up as she spoke. 'It's a bit of a hike without a wagon, but we can do it if renegades don't attack us while we're travelling. Once we return, all will be well.'

Josie stepped over a piece of rusting wreckage heaped by the edge of the trail. It was the remains of a bandit she had killed last year, after a gang had tried to knock over the bank to steal a new shipment of capacitors. The droid had customized himself with wheels to replace his legs, as had the rest of the gang, but those wheels had not made them able to outrun her swift horse and swifter bullets. Their weather-worn carcasses dotted the hillside, much picked away by crows scavenging for usable salvage. Josie regarded the ruined hulk for a moment with savage satisfaction, and then her thoughts grew grim as she considered Ella's words. 'I've heard tell for people like us the City is death, nothing more, nothing less.'

'It isn't so!' The old android shook her head in vehement denial. 'You heard wrong. The City is the final best place for all of us. We've been talking about returning for the last five years. Losing our homestead just made the decision easier.' Ella looked down at Josie, her stern voice turning quiet. 'You're a decent sort, Sheriff, why don't you come with us? Droids are returning, more and more of them. Haven't you noticed? We could use someone like you to protect us on the journey. We're a fair piece from the City; it'll take maybe a couple weeks to get there since we've got to match the pace of the slowest.'

Josie thought this over for a time as she walked beside Paint, her boots crunching through the gravel and raising a soft puff of dust with each stride. Behind her she could hear the rest of the party as they trudged along. Some spoke quietly, but for the most part they walked in silence, passive, accepting of their fate. Everything Josie had heard about the City had been bad. It was a place of uniformity, with no room for individuality — or the misfit. Droids like her with an autonomous mind were not accepted. According to legend, this was the reason why Josie's ancestors had left the City and sought a new life and a new fate out in the world beyond the City's enormous sprawl.

She had no idea why people who had lived independently and known no other existence were upping and leaving for a place where they would be forced to change, if not killed outright. She considered her words carefully, mindful of the child's youth and the sensibilities of the adults still smarting from their losses.

'Thank you for the offer, ma'am, but I can't go with you. I'm needed here in Cayuse. This place is my life, my friends are here, and everything I care about.' Reaching out a hand, she patted Paint's shoulder, sheathed in bunched hydraulics, feeling the strength under her fingers as his limbs worked smoothly. 'Besides, out here, there are horses.'

Ella sighed heavily. 'I was afraid of that, but never mind. It's going to take us a couple days to get everything together for the journey. If you change your mind, Sheriff Josie, you know where to find us.'

'I won't forget.'

✿

Josie found the concept of return haunting her thoughts. She saw the family fairly often, both Ella and her husband Virgil, as well as their adult children, and the one grandchild, who she learned was named Ruby. Once they had been settled in the local hotel, they occupied themselves with their preparations for departure, drawing upon the savings they had at the local bank, and performing odd jobs to acquire the necessary gear for the trip.

The news of the family's plans to return to the City spread through the town. Much to Josie's surprise, many people were not only willing to help Ella's family prepare for the journey, but made up their minds on the instant to travel with them. Before long it seemed as if half the town was packing wagons, and doing their best to acquire oxen, the small traction engines that pulled wagons and carts.

A week after meeting the family, from the window of her office in the well-weathered City Hall, Josie watched the streets bustle with activity as people packed and prepared. Her nerves felt twitchy with the need to do something, and yet the rate of reported crimes had gone down. Even some of the hardcases and known criminals seemed to have caught the yearning to return to the City and had left the territory.

'Nothing much doing here,' she muttered, rising from her chair. 'Guess I'll make a patrol and see if anything is happening elsewhere.' Pushing open the door, she nearly tripped over Ruby. She had been standing just outside the office, small hands clasped together in front of her.

'Ruby! What are you doing here? Is anything wrong?' Josie knelt to put her head more on a level with that of the smaller droid and spoke gently.

'I wanted to ask you, Sheriff, if I could,' Ruby's voice trailed off uncertainly. 'Grandma and Grandpa wouldn't want me to ask this, but I had to, so I snuck away.' She threw a guilty glance over her shoulder, but the corridor was empty of watchful relatives.

'Sure, Ruby. Ask me anything. Well, almost anything,' she amended hastily. Some things were better left to parents or grandparents for explanations.

Ruby's blue optics brightened. 'Can I ride your Paint horse again? He's wonderful.'

*

After tracking down old Virgil to ask his permission, Josie collected Paint, saddled him up, and boosted Ruby onto his back. After warning them both sternly about keeping to the town limits, she sent them off.

'You trust that horse, do you?' said Virgil, watching as Paint loped gently up Main Street with his small passenger.

'Of course I do! He's savvy as anybody and my partner to boot. He's the one that sensed your presence and dug you folk out of your hidey-hole. You might've been under the ashes and debris for a long time if it wasn't for him.'

The old droid grunted and nodded. 'Is that so? Then he's a lot smarter than most of the mechanical critters we've got around here.'

Josie smiled. 'Doc Gabriel built him — he's the best builder in the territory. He used to be the town's only doctor, but now that we've got Doc Jones and Doc Griffin, he's pretty much retired from patching busted up miners and people shot fulla holes in fights.' She looked at the older droid and her light tone grew serious. 'He could help Ruby grow up, when the time is right. He's the only one I'd trust to do that kind of delicate work.'

'Thanks, Sheriff, but no thanks. Outlaws killed Ruby's parents, my son an' daughter-in-law; they were the ones who insisted on making a child in this dangerous time. Ruby isn't going to need any mods, she isn't going to grow up or be anything more than what she is now. She's coming with us to the City and they'll take care of her like they'll take care of all of us.' He turned away.

Josie grabbed at his arm, catching the sleeve of his work shirt as he stomped off. 'They'll kill you! Or worse! Listen to me, dammit!' The sleeve tore: the old man kept going as if he couldn't hear her. Her hands knotted above the grips of her pistols then slowly relaxed. The sad fact was that Virgil was not breaking any law she knew of, whether written or unwritten, and if she believed in that law, there was nothing she could legally do to stop him. She vented coolant in a soft groan.

Turning on her heel, Josie strode rapidly through the town, leaving Main Street and traveling along a succession of side streets and alleyways. Cayuse was not a large town; soon the business district gave way to a succession of machine shops and forges. At last she stopped outside a large building hard by the salvage yard. A weathered and rusty sign above the wide doors stated simply: Gabriel — Repairs — All Sorts.

The interior of the establishment was cool and dark. Josie waited for a moment to give her optics time to adjust to the lower level of lighting. Once that was done, she walked inside, closing the door behind her. The shop looked like nothing more than a warehouse, heaped high with parts. Many were corralled neatly in boxes and bins, but capacitors, diodes, microcomponents, and chips were scattered across counter tops like dusty jewels and exotic insects, gleaming in the soft light filtering from the back of the shop. Josie stepped carefully as the narrow way between the shelves and bins was half-clogged with power cables, conduit, and connectors. She smiled internally at the sight. 'I see things haven't changed much,' she murmured.

'Welcome, Josie Two Guns. I'm back here. Come and see my latest project.' The baritone voice was warm and masculine, holding an undercurrent of excitement.

It took a little time, but eventually Josie picked her way into the back of the shop, where a series of work tables were illuminated by bright mobile lamps. The air was clean and tinged with the faint smell of solder and new electronics. Small specialized robots swarmed over a large form lying motionless atop the very large central worktable.

'Here you are at last. Feast your eyes on this. You at least should appreciate it.' Gabriel spread out his hands over the surface of the worktable, gently shooing the spider-like assembly 'bots. 'Go on now, let Josie have a look.' They scampered obediently out of the way.

Gabriel was taller than Josie, but thin. He hadn't bothered to make himself overly robust, opting instead for nimbleness and an extra pair of arms situated below the first pair. When not in use, those arms were often folded neatly at his sides, with the hands clasped in front of him, but now they gestured in counterpoint to his primary pair of arms. He wore overalls covered with many pockets, each pocket bulging with either tools, parts, or both. His optics were constantly shifting colour, the result of multiple layers of specialized lenses that gave him enhanced vision for micro-work.

'You've been away too long, Josie. I've made a lot of progress!' Gabriel pointed his beak of a metal nose at the project. 'Well?'

❊

'Will it hurt, do you think, when we get to the City and they take us in?' Ruby asked as they traversed the edge of the town. Corrals of oxen waited, shut down for now, but soon to be activated to pull the wagons on their pilgrimage.

I don't know, thought Paint as he walked along a dusty side street. *And I'll never know, because I'm not going to the City. I'm staying right here with Josie.* Not that Ruby could hear: she'd never been equipped with a wireless link. Animals were not typically capable of speaking aloud, and few people knew of his connection to his partner. Sign language would have to suffice. With a snort, he turned his head to look at Ruby and rocked his head in a definite negative.

'You're not going?' Ruby sat bolt upright in the saddle. 'But Grandpa says it's where all droids belong.'

Paint snorted again, shaking his head and neck for emphasis, the vibration traveling through his frame.

'But I thought you'd be going with us.' Ruby leaned forward to stretch her skinny upper body along Paint's neck, turning sideways in the saddle to avoid the saddle horn. Almost in the same breath, she added, 'Why wouldn't you belong in the City? If it's where all droids came from, I mean?'

Paint stopped in the middle of the street, thinking hard. Turning, he picked up a lope, heading toward the west side of town. Ruby hung on tightly.

*

It took a number of qualities to build horses — patience and cybernetic skill being two of the most necessary — but even more than those prerequisites, it required an artist's heart. Gabriel of Cayuse was an artist; every creature he produced proclaimed it.

Josie looked down at the cybernetic equine on the table. 'She's a beauty, Gabriel. Before today I'd have said Paint was your best, but this one is . . .' She passed her hands over it, at a loss for words. The horse in question was matte black in color, although her coat had a subtle iridescence in the light of the lamps. Her form was graceful, with smooth, elegant lines. 'She looks like she'll be fast.'

'Aye, fast as the wind, I'm hoping. I made some design improvements to the internal mechanism.' Gabriel stabbed a finger down at the exposed cables in one of the forelegs. 'And see here.' He used his two right hands to stroke the horse's neck and back simultaneously. 'I've integrated solar arrays under her hide from ears to tail. Even a rider and saddle won't block out all the sunlight. During the daylight hours she'll build a charge that she can use for a boost or to run at night. I've got the usual power supply in her, too, but the sun is free energy. I'm anxious to see how it works for her.'

'That's a great idea,' said Josie, spirits lifting a little at Gabriel's enthusiasm. 'How soon can you start her up?'

'No brain for her, yet,' he sighed, patting the black horse's head. 'Her skull's mostly empty and that's a fact. It's the hardest component to find, and the most important, of course,' said Gabriel. 'I'm very picky about the brain—you've got to have the right kind of character, you see.'

'Where will you get one?' Josie found gazing at the half-constructed form of the cybernetic horse was starting to make her feel slightly nauseated. She knew very well all of them had been built in a similar fashion, but since she had no memories of that process, seeing it before her like this was discomforting.

'I don't know. I scratch-built much of what went into Paint. For the needed CPU components I had to send off to the industrial town of Germanium, and it took forever for everything to get in.' Gabriel shook his head sadly. 'The manufacturing heart of Germanium was destroyed by a big fight between two rival gangs of outlaws two years ago. Last I heard, pretty much all the people decided to return to the City after that, so now the place is practically a ghost town. A pity, the builders and smiths there did first-rate work.' He patted the horse's head again. 'I don't want to buy salvage off the junkers—any CPU they're selling would likely be from an outlaw.'

'So where will you get the brain for this new horse if not from them?' asked Josie.

Moving to the recumbent droid's hindquarters, Gabriel began to work on the exposed inner connections of ceramic bone and flexible hydraulics. 'I don't know. Maybe I'll take a trip to find another industrial town that's still producing. I'm sure the Maker will provide something when the time is right.'

'I hope so,' said Josie. 'You may be running out of time, though. Looks like half the people of Cayuse are going to be following Virgil and his family to the City.'

Gabriel shrugged. 'Doesn't matter. You've got to be strong to live free. The City calls to those who can't, drawing them to itself. People come and people go from Cayuse. If they leave now, eventually new ones will come here.' Lifting his head, he looked into Josie's face directly, eyes shifting in colour from amber to blue as he adjusted the lenses. 'Or else I'll build them.'

Josie left the shop to watch many of the residents of Cayuse pack, but for once her thoughts were of beginnings and not of endings.

❉

Inside the pelvic girdle of the horse, Gabriel began to make a final sequence of connections, patient and painstaking. Slowly the sensation of being watched intruded into the happy haze of concentration in which he wrapped himself. Lifting his tools from the work area, he looked up. A pair of blue optics framed by copper tresses peered at him over the far edge of the table.

'Hullo. Paint brought me here. I think maybe you can answer a question I asked him.'

'Paint's a sensible fellow,' Gabriel replied, putting down his tools. 'What question?'

'If all droids came from the City, why wouldn't a horse like Paint want to go there?'

'It's not where horses were designed.' Gabriel shifted the lenses in his eyes, bringing the child into better focus. 'The City might have droids of all types, but nothing like Paint or any animals. The City never imagined them. Animals are made out here, from our dreams, by droids like us.'

'You mean someone here made Paint?' Ruby ran her fingers over the black metal shell of the partly-finished horse on the table.

'Sure. I did,' said Gabriel. 'Just like I'm making that one you're touching.'

'What?' Ruby stared up at the old droid then lowered her gaze to fully look at the table in front of her. 'Ooo.' There was a long silence while Ruby took in the form of the horse. At last she spoke in a hushed voice.

'Can you make me a horse?'

'Hmm, that depends, young one. First, who are you?'

'I'm Ruby of the Red Ore family. My folks and grandparents had a mining stake out beyond Coaltown.' She thought for a moment, pulling at the front of her pinafore. 'The outlaws stole our ingots and burned the house down. My parents are dead, and my grandparents and relatives are going back to the City.' She lifted her head and focused on him, looking closely at his face. 'Who're you, sir?'

'I'm Gabriel, Builder of Horses.' Gabriel lowered his voice to a conspiratorial whisper. 'You know what they are, don't you?'

'Horses? They're wonderful,' said Ruby at once. 'And beautiful.'

'So they are, but they're more than that, child.' He leaned toward Ruby. 'Let me tell you . . . '

✿

The wagon train was assembled, taking up nearly the length of the main street of Cayuse. Virgil's large family, their wagons and oxen headed the train, and made up nearly a third of those departing for the City. The rest were people from Cayuse and the surrounding territory. All was in readiness, except for one detail. Ruby had gone missing. Virgil stood with his chest nearly touching Josie's own, his body tense with anger and fear. 'You're the law 'round here, find her!'

'Maybe she's decided she doesn't want to go off and die,' said Josie mildly, ignoring the implied insult in the man's words. Upset people rarely bothered to watch their language and Virgil was no exception.

'She's not old enough to make that decision,' Virgil growled. 'Besides, no one's going to die — the Maker will look after all of us.'

'I think maybe it's been too long since you raised kids. She may be more mature than you think.' Josie held up a hand to shut off the torrent of angry language. 'Save your energy and get your company moving. You're wasting daylight. Paint and I will check the town. If we find Ruby; we'll bring her to you. It's not as if you'll get that far ahead of us in half a day.'

Somewhat mollified, the older droid reluctantly put his wagon train in motion, no longer able to resist the insistent urge to return to the City. Josie found her spotted mount and began a painstaking search of Cayuse, checking all the places that Ruby had been known to frequent during her stay in town. Several hours later, with the sun well past noon, Josie admitted defeat and turned her horse's nose toward the trail taken by Virgil and the wagon train. Paint's swift gallop eventually brought them up on the dusty column of vehicles and people.

'Well, where is she?' Had it been capable, Virgil's glare would have killed her dead on the spot.

'I've searched everywhere; I couldn't find her.' Josie wiped the dust from her face with her neckerchief.

'That's not a good answer, Sheriff.' Josie found herself looking down the open end of a very large double-barrelled gun. She had no idea where Virgil had gotten the weapon, but it was the sort used to blow apart heavily modified desperados, and the way he was waving it around put more fear into her then it would have in the hands of a proper outlaw. 'Put that thing away before you hurt someone with it,' she said coolly, deliberately not reaching for her own pistol. A horse neighed, the sound thin and sweet on the hot desert breeze. Paint flicked his metal ears. Virgil ignored it.

'You said you'd bring her.'

'I said I'd bring her if I could find her,' Josie corrected him. 'Paint and I turned Cayuse upside-down; we couldn't find a trace of her.' She looked at the line of vehicles. 'Are you sure she isn't asleep in one of the wagons?'

'No. She isn't with us, and that means you've got her.'

'I don't —'

BOOM! Fire leaped from the end of the gun, the shock of the blast blowing Josie off her horse to the ground, her right arm gone, leaving a ragged metal stump above the elbow. Bits of fizzing wire sparked until her autonomic systems shut down the power to the limb. Several of the women screamed. Paint shrieked in fury, but the threat of the gun held him at bay. A sound like drumbeats thumped in the background under the cacophony of shouts and curses from the watching people. Virgil ignored them, keeping the gun aimed at Josie. 'The second shot'll take your head off, Sheriff. Where's Ruby?'

A pair of flashing black-metal hooves sent the weapon flying from Virgil's hands. An ebony horse had appeared in time to stop him, crushing the smoking weapon underfoot as if it were a snake. The animal moved with such smoothness that even in the midst of her shock, Josie recognized her at once as Gabriel's project brought to vibrant life.

How, she thought in a daze, *how did he manage? He said he didn't have a brain for the horse, yet.*

She has mine. The thoughts broke in over the same link Josie shared with Paint. *Sheriff Josie, speak to Grandfather for me.*

Josie took a closer look. Bright against the darkness of the horse's outer shell, long threads of copper red gleamed among the worked metal filaments of her mane. When Josie was fairly sure she had her voice under control, she said. 'Virgil, I've found Ruby.'

'What?' Virgil stared around wildly in a vain search for his granddaughter, thoughts of combat momentarily abandoned. 'Where?'

'Right here.' Josie pointed her remaining hand at Ruby.

Virgil's mouth dropped open in shock as he stared at the graceful equine droid.

'No. How did you . . . ?' Virgil floundered about as he tried to understand his grandchild's shift in form and function. 'Ruby, what have you done to yourself?'

'She's been to see Doc Gabriel. I'm not sure how she found out about him, but they must have come to some agreement, and so he made her into one of his horses.' Josie pulled herself into a sitting position and looked up at Ruby. 'Am I right?' The horse nodded her head.

That's right. Gabriel needed a mind for this body, and so . . .

'Stop this nonsense, child, and come with us.' Not being privy to the conversation, Virgil made a grab for the horse's neck, but Ruby evaded him easily. Quickly she wove through the wagon train, touching the members of her family with her nose, returning at last to touch Virgil as well.

Arching her neck and tail proudly, Ruby galloped off into the ocher hills without a backward glance.

Virgil looked after Ruby for a minute. 'Silly girl. Surely she'll follow us once she comes to her senses.' He turned away from Josie, got the group of travelers back into order, and sent them moving down the road toward the distant promise of the City.

Josie climbed to her feet and steadied herself against Paint. Once she had regained her balance, she gathered up the remains of her shattered arm and stowed it carefully in a saddlebag. No one had offered to help, and she wasn't about to push the point with a pack of droids obsessed with returning to the City.

'I'm sure Gabriel won't mind a little more work this night, seeing as how I took the damage on his behalf,' she said ruefully, climbing into the saddle with the aid of her remaining arm. Once mounted, she watched the procession until they were out of sight.

At last Paint turned his head a little to bring Josie into view of one eye. *Shall we go back to Cayuse now and get you fixed up? I guess it's going to be a bit quieter for a time.*

'I don't know about it being quiet my friend, but yes, let's go home.' Paint moved into a ground-eating lope; after a time the outskirts of Cayuse appeared on the horizon, the buildings forming dark silhouettes against the setting sun.

'Whatever possessed Ruby to want to become a horse?' Josie suddenly spoke the thoughts she had been pondering during the return trip.

I like being a horse, said Paint. *It's a perfectly nice shape and I like being your partner.*

'Yes, but you were made that way from the beginning, Ruby started out as a two-legged person — not that you're not a *person* I mean, but her new form is such a change from what she was.' She shifted in the saddle restlessly. 'I'm not saying this right. It's not like Gabriel kidnapped her, I'm sure of that, but what did he say to her? She left her family. That must've been hard.'

I understand. Perhaps Gabriel simply told her about horses.

Josie sat up straight, remembering something Ruby had said. 'Horses. What are horses then?'

Ruby's wild whinny echoed faintly down the canyon to them.
I think you know.

Josie clapped her heels to Paint's sides, and he leaped into motion, galloping at reckless speed down the main street of Cayuse, leaving a trail of dust burning red in the evening haze.

'Perhaps I do!' she shouted, over the thunder of hoof beats.

Perfection

WILL ISGROVE *and* JON GARRAD

ELDRITCH LIMPED DOWN THE HILL AND OUT ON TO ANOTHER STRETCH of rock-strewn desert floor. He knew he had at least another month of travel before he reached the village Isabelle mentioned in her last letter, but his limp was slowing him down: more likely it would take twice the time. His power levels were dropping, and the limp was proving a drain. He only hoped the village was large enough to have a parts shop . . .

The reasons had been slight, though the fight had been unavoidable. The droids in Tanktown had been openly hostile toward him since he had walked into the saloon there. The reception had been colder than in any other town he had visited since his journey began seven years ago. He'd a feeling the inhabitants of the village he hoped to arrive at soon would be even less happy to see him; they'd probably be more aggressive too. Eldritch hoped not. If he took many more bullets, he'd be a goner.

His memory storage had been damaged in the fight: he couldn't quite piece together the whole of the shoot-out. At first he couldn't even remember why he had started on this journey, why he had decided to head out onto the frontier and into the deserts beyond. He had known only a curious kind of dread; a creeping sense that he had lost something very precious. Then he'd found the letters, and his recovery program had kicked in, restoring the saved memories of the last seven years. The only memories lost permanently, it seemed, were his last moments in Tanktown, and judging by his injuries, that was fairly self-explanatory. As he walked, Eldritch ran a diagnostic, trying to remember . . .

✾

Eldritch had come across the rough collection of buildings and statue of some local notary making up Tanktown half a year after setting out from Morgantown. Tanktown was just the right side of run-down, though Eldritch didn't think it would be too long before the term 'ramshackle' became more applicable. It was quite a contrast to the clean and well-kept buildings and streets in Morgantown.

He wasn't sure of the place at all. The droids he had passed on his way to the saloon had all nodded to him, but Eldritch suspected there was little courtesy in the gesture. None of them had said a word: even the barkeep had been silent as he showed Eldritch to the room where he lay, running his recovery program.

Eldritch carried his memories with him in crystal cells. The system was considered an inelegant second to internal memory drives, but Eldritch found it more trustworthy, and besides, he had the advantage of compatibility . . .

He pulled the old seven-crystal cell from his coat and turned it over, reflecting. It was one of the oldest he'd ever seen: possibly over a hundred years old. Each crystal carried only a single memory: letters from someone called Isabelle to someone called Method.

The letters told a story, but it was fragmented. Eldritch was only certain that Isabelle and Method had once been together and living in Lennontown. Then one day Isabelle had left. None of the letters Eldritch had found explained her disappearance much beyond it being something she 'had to do'. Method had set out in pursuit of her, but for seven letters at least, had not found her. Eldritch had found no replies from Method; it looked as though Isabelle had left a trail of messages in an effort to dissuade him at every step of the way.

The desire to follow the letters had taken him quite by surprise. It seemed that from the moment he read the first letter he was compelled to track them down. He had never felt so curious about anything else in his life. The mystery of Isabelle's disappearance enthralled him. His few friends had often joked that his curiosity was a flaw in his circuitry. Maybe it was, but Eldritch found himself unable to resist trying to track the letters down and find Isabelle and Method.

Eldritch gathered his belongings and headed downstairs. He nodded curtly to the barkeep and briefly considered another attempt at conversation, but decided against it. He didn't think it too wise to antagonise the townsfolk anymore than he had to; he also didn't think it would take much for them to become aggressive. Ignoring the barkeep's answering glare, Eldritch left the saloon, looking for whatever passed for a library in Tanktown. The last four letters he had found, the ones in the towns out on the frontier, had all been located in the libraries of the respective towns. Eldritch walked up to the dull grey building and through the door.

The droid at the desk was small and just as dull looking as the building. She was also just as unhelpful and rude as the barkeep, and it took all Eldritch's control to keep from shouting as he tried to talk his way into her archives. She asked where he was from, and was quite obviously sure he was lying. What was his business here? That took the best part of an hour to explain, and the story he had prepared for just such an occasion was summarily dismissed. No droids came travelling this far west anymore; everyone was leaving for the City in the east.

Eldritch had indeed passed a number of droids heading in the opposite direction to him. They were mostly younger droids, and those few that stopped to talk to him all said they were heading to the City. They refused to tell him why, and he didn't press; after all, he was following a series of letters written almost one hundred years ago for no real reason save curiosity. Did he really have a right to judge?

Eventually, the librarian gave in and surrendered the archive key, allowing Eldritch into the library proper to begin his search. He made his way down to a skylit cellar, turning out every box and searching every drawer, turning over every stack of paper in search of one darkly shining crystal square. As always when he found himself close to another letter, he began to worry that the crystal would elude him; that the trail would go cold and he would be left with nowhere to go.

The sun had vanished from the skylight by the time Eldritch eventually found the crystal, buried in the bowels of a chest marked 'Sundries and Effects'. Fighting back the temptation to download it there and then, he slipped it into his coat with the others and made his way upstairs, not wanting to outstay his dubious welcome from the librarian. She was no longer behind her desk when Eldritch emerged: with that, he he knew trouble was coming his way. Laying a hand on his holster, he crept to the window, looked out and swore.

Standing in front of the library were three droids: he recognised two as patrons of the inn, and the third had the look of a sheriff about him. The innkeeper was standing in his doorway on the other side of the street, enjoying a good view of the show about to be played out. Eldritch signed, kept one hand on his gun and stepped out.

'Howdy there, sheriff.' It wasn't a great line, and it probably just made them angrier, but Eldritch really didn't think he would talk his way out of what was to follow. He nodded to the two deputies. No one replied: they just opened fire on him. Bullets sparked and clanged off him as he ducked back into the library, away from the flying lead, and drew his own pistol. 'All this for asking a few questions?' he said to himself.

His chest was scratched and had a few dents in it already; one good hit would go right through him. He waited for a break in the shooting and then dived through the doorway, firing two shots; direct hits to the sheriff's chest. As the sheriff fell backwards, Eldritch rolled smoothly to his feet and bolted for the statue in the town square, snapping off another shot at a deputy as he took cover.

They'd reloaded by the time he did so, and let loose a firestorm of their own. Bullets winged off in all directions; a lucky ricochet caught him in the side of the head, rattling his circuits. Snarling, Eldritch rose and fired between the statue's legs; two more shots split the deputies, sending them ducking for cover themselves.

At a guess, he reasoned they'd get on either side of the statue and shred him in a cross fire. Eldritch threw himself forward, rolled and sprinted for the saloon. His last shot took the barkeep down — direct hit on a knee joint — and he was through the doors in a second, diving for the bar as the last of the deputies' bullets tore what was left of the doors from their hinges.

The two deputies entered the inn cautiously, barrels smoking, and as Eldritch peeked around the bar, he realised one had unslung a shotgun from somewhere. They were serious about wanting him dead, and the sight of him drew a blast that took the bartop apart and practically blew a hole through the wall where his head had been before he ducked.

On his back, Eldritch drew his second gun and fired, eyes whirring in a struggle to pierce the smoke and settling debris. The deputy with the shotgun went down, his neck blown away and his head hanging by a few wires. The other hurled himself backward, but Eldritch had the advantage now and followed the droid's trajectory, firing all the time as he rolled to his feet. The droid landed out in the street with a neat hole in the centre of his head.

Eldritch picked up on the click of the shotgun being cocked, but he reacted just too late. Even as he dove for cover, he felt his right leg come apart at the knee, felt the wires tear and coolant lines sunder as the limb fell somewhere behind him. The backlash went to Eldritch's central processor, turning his vision photonegative and shorting out almost every process he had left. The barkeep didn't get the chance for a second shot; Eldritch's reflexes put a bullet in his central power unit and shut him down for good before eventually giving in to system failure.

*

His thoughts came back to him in fragments. First his identity: then the insistent buzz of his diagnostic systems telling of the damage he had taken; then the sense of loss, and the fear that came with it. Eldritch was no mechanic, and the best he could do with his leg was make it take his weight. Anything faster than a shuffle, and it'd probably be gone altogether.

He was out of Tanktown by dawn, using the shotgun as a crutch, the newest letter loaded into his memory port. That'd tell him where to go; he could worry about restoring his own cells on the journey. What mattered was finding Isabelle, and someone to fix up his leg.

*

The letter had led him into the desert, he remembered. It hadn't provided much detail on Isabelle's desired destination, nor had it shed any more light on her motives. The only real gain, aside from a direction to head in, was the certainty that Eldritch was still on the right track.

His compass was malfunctioning slightly: he found himself having to climb high dunes to double-check directions, which was not an ideal situation. His leg seized momentarily, and he stumbled and fell half way down one dune. The fall rattled him, and caused a few tertiary systems to begin playing up. Eventually, he was forced to deactivate his guidance unit completely and rely on the sun, his vision being the only sense still functioning anything close to reliably.

The sky was beginning to darken, and Eldritch figured a big storm was approaching. They had storms back west, but they were fairly rare, and mostly quite calm compared to the raging storms he'd heard had dogged the migration. It dawned on Eldritch that the storms were said to be worse the further west one headed – he'd been built to handle rough conditions, but he wasn't exactly running at full potential, and he was heading into unknown territory. He could only hope he would be under cover when his leg finally gave out.

As the day slogged by, he wondered if Isabelle and Method had been caught in a storm along this route. He wasn't happy with the thought their journeys may have ended there, against the rain and the lightning.

By nightfall, he found himself trekking through a wide, deep canyon. The path he was following through it was largely clear of obstruction: a blessed relief to his degrading leg, and less drain on his power levels. He still felt he had enough in reserve to reach the next town, which he hoped he would find at the other end of the canyon.

The storm finally looked ready to break, and there was no place to shelter, as far as he could see in the gloom. The canyon trail began to curve to the left and rise gently at first then with increasing steepness. Heavy rain would turn the canyon floor into a river. Eldritch needed somewhere to shelter, and picked his way up the slope a little way, looking for a cave, for a boulder, for anything he could scramble under until the storm passed.

Rain was beginning to fall heavily when he reached a small rockslide, with — thank the Maker — a cave near the top. Visibility would have been low even if his vision was running at capacity, but looking up at the cave, he was struck by how much like a mouth it looked. The rock around it almost looked like features of some huge sculpted face.

Eldritch didn't waste any more time thinking about this, and began to drag his damaged frame over the slick rock and up toward the cave. His right leg was next to useless, but he found he had enough strength and balance in his other limbs to scale the cliff side and drag himself into the cave.

The small opening gave way to a large low cave. Sheltered from the worst of the rain, Eldritch rested his back against the far wall of the cave and shut down every system he could spare, even his failing eyes. His core processor, ticking over in the long dark, re-read the letter from Isabelle. It would pass the time.

❋

Dearest Method,

I must plead again that you call off your pursuit of me. The road I now must take is long and dangerous, and I would fear for your safety should you follow me.

You know I cannot tell you the reasons why, and I must again say this is my choice to make and I must see it through without you. There has not been a day passed by that I have not thought of you. But you are wasting yourself chasing me. Please let me go.

You really must turn back, you were not made for this life; you have greater things to achieve than destruction in the desert trying to reach me. The village I seek should not been seen by the likes of you.

I do not know what will happen to me when I reach the end, but if there is any chance of returning to you I will. You must believe that. This calling is not yours to answer. If you would truly do anything to see me happy as you once claimed, do this. Turn back now.

Please do this. For me.

Your only Isabelle.

❉

Eldritch's systems reactivated. The rest had done him good; his vision seemed to be stabilising again. He lurched forward, just in time to see a rifle bullet thump into the roof of the cave. With a grunt, he dropped to his front and crawled forward.

The sky overhead was a clear blue, and the clouds of the storm could be seen far away toward the eastern horizon. Below him, the canyon steamed in the heat of the sun. Another bullet struck rock close to his hand. *Whoever's shooting ain't half as accurate as those goons in Tanktown,* he thought absently as he drew his pistol.

He estimated the sniper's reload time and waited for another shot. When it came, the bullet struck about two feet from where Eldritch lay. He rose and fired three rounds into the canyon, expertly tracing the shots back to a narrow area on the far side. He dropped out of sight and waited. Moments passed without a reply shot. He was about to creep forward when another rifle fired.

The shot came from a different direction and was far more accurate. Had Eldritch been a little higher up, the bullet would have taken his head apart. He pulled himself back into the safety of the cave as two more thudded into the rock behind him: and that was when he saw the clock.

It was a simple analogue clock, with a dull silver face. The mechanisms were visible behind the face, various larger gears turning various smaller ones. The clock was set in the stone of the cave wall and, Eldritch realised, was silent. It was authentic clockwork — an antique.

There were no other markings on the wall, just the silver clock, ticking silently away. A bullet chipped the wall to the left of Eldritch, but he ignored it, leaning forward, fascinated by the whirr of the gears. The time the clock was keeping didn't match up to his internal clock. Suddenly and in complete silence, the cogs and wheels began to speed up, the hands spinning round faster and faster.

'In the cave,' a voice shouted, 'you are in violation of sacred ground! If you do not step down this minute, you will be destroyed!' Eldritch was too enthralled by the clock to pay too much attention. What did grab him, though, was the low rumble that was beginning to sound all around him.

Another shot was fired, but the sound was lost amid the creaking and groaning. The clock spun faster. The floor trembled below him and he felt the curious sensation that the floor of the cave was rising up to meet the ceiling.

The clock burst apart: cogs flew across the cave, one striking Eldritch on the arm and sticking fast. The floor was rising up: if he wasn't quick, he was going to join the mess of clock parts. He turned away, but something caught his eye. The hole where the clock had been was empty now and he could see to the back wall. Inside was a white sign with black lettering, fixed to the rock. It read simply: WAY OUT.

The cave was fast disappearing and Eldritch limped toward the cave mouth. Another bullet struck the rock. If he guessed right, the second rifle would be out of ammunition. Eldritch tensed his good leg and dived. Firing several rounds into the rocks around the cave, Eldritch crashed against the rockslide and rolled to the canyon floor under the cover of the dust. His right leg groaned as he clambered behind a boulder, braced his arm and waited for the dust to clear.

'Drop your weapon and cease hostilities, or we will destroy you.' It was the same voice that had warned him about sacred ground. Turning to the direction of the voice, Eldritch counted seventeen droids lining the canyon on either side. All of them were training rifles on him. Eldritch knew he was good, but good enough to take down seventeen droids with eight bullets, on a faulty leg?

He threw down his gun, and the droids descended. They walked unsteadily on the rough ground, slipping occasionally or stumbling; they were old, plainly designed, with clumsy gyros and thick limbs.

They placed him in the centre of the column as they marched him through the rest of the canyon. He was worried at first that the pace they set would be too much for his battered frame to keep up with, but it soon transpired that these droids weren't at all mobile. Even when the canyon path flattened out they struggled to make much progress.

They marched on for three days. At night the droids would gather into a group and, aside from two guards and a watcher, they shut down until sunrise. It looked as though they needed to, regardless of system damage or the lack of it: Eldritch had no fixed objection to the practice when it was necessary, but it was by no means a regular thing for him or any droid he knew. Just how old were these droids?

The morning of the fourth day saw the column climb slowly out of the canyon, into a dilapidated circle of small huts. He had his doubts about the presence of a parts shop or mechanic; the droids had said nothing to him during the journey, and didn't seem the type to offer help to strangers. Whoever they were, they were not going to tell him. He tried to identify the one who had spoken earlier, but there was little to distinguish between them all.

As they filed into the village, the droids around him melted away until only two were left. He considered putting up resistance, maybe snatching at one of their guns, but it seemed pointless. They had kept him alive for some reason, he might as well find out why: and maybe, he realised, this was the village Isabelle had written of.

The other droids, those who filed away from the column, were going back to varieties of strange and pointless business. One droid was simply walking endlessly between two huts, forward and back. How long he had been at it Eldritch couldn't guess, but he had created deep ruts in the sandy earth. Another was laying tiles in a large circle, while another droid picked the tiles up and put them back on the pile. The circle would never be more than half-complete.

Eldritch's guards led him to a small hut no different to all the others around him. They indicated he go inside, but made no move to follow him. They just stood there. Eldritch pushed open the hut door, which squeaked on its hinges, and stepped inside.

A trapdoor took up most of the floor space, large, square and grey, but in the far corner of the hut sat a solitary droid. Beside him was a small heap of ancient circuit boards. Every now and then the droid would pick up a board and begin to work on it. Eldritch stood fascinated as the droid dropped each board back to the heap and picked another at random, repeating the process.

Eldritch stepped closer to the droid; he was covered in dust. In fact, the whole room was covered in dust, save for Eldritch and the circuit boards. He was curious what would happen if he took the dull green boards away, but decided against it and turned to the trapdoor.

When he dropped it open a thick cloud of dust billowed up. The droid picked up another circuit board and went to work on it, not noticing Eldritch descend the stone stairs the open hatch exposed. He shuffled to the bottom and stepped into a long, low room, at the far end of which was a small wooden table. Rested upon it was the head of a droid.

It had a face and features, like droids of Eldritch's generation, but it looked far older than even the droids in the village above. Despite that, it looked vaguely familiar, though he could not place it. It opened its eyes as he approached, and smiled. Eldritch tried not to betray any shock, but the smile seemed to tell him he had failed. It was an indulgent, arrogant smile, which seemed so out of place on a droid head on a table under the ground.

'Hello, EL631,' the head spoke in a clipped accent that Eldritch couldn't place. 'Don't bother looking for wires, there aren't any.' Eldritch looked back at that self-satisfied smile. 'My name is Maxwell, by the way.'

'Where is this? Why was I brought here?'

The head chuckled and the sound was almost as annoying as the smile. 'This is Candella, EL631, and I believe you wanted to come here.'

'You know of the letters?' he asked slowly.

'I know what you are looking for, yes,' said Maxwell, 'but as I told your predecessor, you can go no further.'

'Why is that?'

'Because, EL631, you are not pure enough. I must say you didn't travel half as well as . . .' The eyes went back in the head and Eldritch heard a faint whirring noise; internal memory, which meant quality parts, City-built or scavenged. Given Maxwell's age, he guessed the former to be the case. '. . . Method. But even so, you will have to wait some considerable time before we deem you worthy of a place in the paradise. So sorry.'

Eldritch stared at the head for sometime before he spoke. 'You know of the letters?' he said finally.

'No.'

'Then how do you know why I'm here?'

'Only four other droids have arrived here who have not been called by us, all of them with the same story. It seems logical that you would be similarly motivated.'

'And where are they?'

Maxwell the head grinned. 'You have already met Method, I believe? The charming fellow at the top of the stairs? The others are about somewhere, I'm sure.'

'What are they doing?'

'Preparing themselves. Waiting until they are allowed to proceed.'

Eldritch realised where it was that he had seen the face.

'The face in the canyon. It's you, isn't it?'

The head took this in its stride. 'I'm a copy of it, rather. In keeping with this place, that too has fallen to ruin. It used to do my job, but as is the way with all things, it joined the others in perfection.'

'What is your job?'

'I guide those droids lucky enough to be called. If they are ready, I grant them permission to proceed. If they are not, like Method upstairs, I tell them to wait and prepare, and, when they are ready, they may join the others.'

Eldritch fingered his gun as a growing sense of dread grew over him. 'How do they prepare?'

'They must become perfect,' said Maxwell, 'through the removal of all unnecessary attachments.'

'What do you mean? All the droids I saw up there were broken.'

'They were perfect. You know all this. That's why you haven't joined the others in the City. The dark City, spreading over the land like oil.'

Eldritch hadn't joined the other young droids from his town in their journey to the City. He'd been more curious about Isabelle and Method than he had been about some supposed land of opportunity over the eastern horizon.

'The City's where you go to find purpose,' he said eventually. 'To do what you were built to do. But what are you offering? Your droids are just doing things mindlessly, for no reason at all.'

'Exactly! They are unified, with one goal together; to reach the perfection of our race.'

'By being broken down? That's not perfection. We have to advance, embrace our new technologies. That's how we become perfect; by moving beyond our design.'

'That way is just perpetual reinvention. We will never be perfect that way. I do not expect you to understand the beauty of this place. Your logic is the very reason you will not be called through for many, many years. You don't even understand yourself; your technology is antiquated. I see you're carrying a crystal memory drive: if novelty is perfection, why do you cling to that?'

Eldritch tried to understand all this. He had followed the letters for a long time, and had faced many obstacles on the road, but with each letter found his obsession had grown a little more. He had so desperately wanted, even needed, to follow them to their conclusion. He would not make the journey back. Candella, if Maxwell was to be believed, would not have any means of manual repair. He wasn't prepared to abide by some foolish commandment about needing to be broken to be let through to whatever lay beyond the town.

What was the mystery? What was it that Maxwell was guarding? What was his idea of perfection? Eldritch knew what he was going to do. He didn't care for this insane little town of malfunctioning droids and this arrogant head. He was going to find Isabelle. Wherever she was, she would answer his two questions. The first, he'd wanted to ask ever since he first read her letter; 'why did you leave?' The second question he had formed only moments ago, but he suspected it was inextricably linked with the first, and that he doubted Maxwell would answer it: 'what is this 'perfection'?'

'I'm going now,' he told Maxwell, 'I'm passing through to whatever dirty secret you hide, and you'd best not try and stop me.'

Maxwell took this calmly. 'I will not try and stop you, EL631, but others might. Those unfortunate enough to still have some conscious thoughts: and the nature of this place is such that where one goes, others will follow.'

Eldritch stopped at the foot of the stairs and turned, 'In the canyon, the clock in the cave up there . . . why did the sign say 'way out'?'

For the first time, Maxwell seemed less than sure of himself. 'Your guess, EL631, is as good as mine. Good day to you.'

*

Back in the small hut, Eldritch lifted the trapdoor shut. The droid with the circuit boards, Method, continued in his pointless labour. Eldritch examined him closer, searching for any sign of activity beyond the reworking of a pile of boards. There was none: he was running on automatic processes. Eldritch waited until Method dropped his current board, and then kicked the pile away. Method's hands fumbled for a board, found nothing but air and dust, and then returned to his lap, and were still.

Eldritch left him to it.

He turned and headed out of the village, back toward the canyon. Behind him he heard the sound of footsteps, and turned around. The droids of Candella, with Method at the front, were lining up. Those without guns carried lengths of wood or metal.

Method spoke, but he did so haltingly, as if he was remembering how to form the words.

'Too pure. Must not pass . . . too pure . . . purify. '

Before Eldritch could fire, Method was charging toward him, crashing into him. The two dropped to the ground and rolled apart. With his leg damaged, Eldritch was by far the slower of the two, at a disadvantage in a fist-fight. Method thumped a fist into Eldritch's face, which sent him sprawling, his vision breaking up again.

In the blur, Method grabbed Eldritch and began to twist at his head, trying to rip it off. Eldritch could hear it creak, feel the joints come apart and the wires stretch. In front of him, he could see his ruined leg, with the ugly hole through it. For some reason it struck him as funny. He had no purchase, no way of throwing Method off. This could be the end . . .

Over Method's shoulder, Eldritch could make out a solitary droid shuffling over, picking up the shotgun and turning it over and over. The droid stood over him and Method.

'Need . . . to . . . purify. Make . . . perfect.' Its voice was dead, empty of all feeling, of all but purpose. It raised its gun and fired, just once.

It took several moments for Eldritch to realise he was still working. His vision occasionally fragmented, and he was getting a lot messages warning of his structural well being not being too well, but he was, essentially, still functioning. The droid with the shotgun stood over him; Method lay atop him, with a smoking hole where his face should have been.

Eldritch pushed Method off and tumbled over, crawling around in the dust. The droids of Candella stood around him, looking down with empty faces. Eldritch tried to stand, but his leg gave out and he fell, looking Method in the smoking hole — and in that moment he understood.

'Nothing but spare parts. Perfection in pieces.' This was the secret; this was perfection for a droid. Eldritch began to understand the simplicity of the idea. They came here and they found oblivion, were saved from an eternity of repair and labour in the City or the strife of surviving out in the desert towns. This was where Isabelle had ended up, and poor Method, who'd loved her enough to give up his sentience for her.

Eldritch realised his body was broken. In another town, he might be repaired, allowed to carry on. If the stories of the City were true, he could be fixed there, given a purpose more meaningful than the mindless routine of the Candella droids. But there was no way to reach the City, or another town. Maxwell's way was the only one left.

Eldritch shut down smiling.

Amanda —

Without whom this book would not be as wonderful as it is. You are my inspiration.

Simon (SP)

Every Sheep Needs A Shepherd

Jeffery Pagenton

THE DROID SLOWED TO A HALT AND SIGHED AS HE LOOKED OUT ACROSS the desert, to the dark shadow on the horizon.

It never seems to get any closer, he thought, lifting his hat to scratch at the rust on his forehead. Wider, over the hours of his journey, expanding to sever the white sands from the sun-bleached sky, but never closer. With another sigh, a deeper one that rattled out from the base of his throat, the droid proceeded to move again.

He was a preacher; it was a calling he'd come to shortly after arriving in the towns, all so long ago. He'd spent his time moving from place to place, helping others to find themselves, bringing them back to good ways when they strayed. Then the towns had begun to empty, and he had discovered that another great migration was underway; that droids everywhere were returning to the City. They were going back to what they had once been, all so long ago.

That was a spiritless life, however. When they had first left the City the droids had been nothing; they had found their purposes out in the towns. When they returned, the preacher knew that they would become nothing again. So he, too, had left, starting back across the desert, back to that distant shadow, the place he had fled all so long ago.

As the sun fell behind him, colouring the sky the same tarnished red as his ageing body, the preacher stopped again. The City was taller in his perspective now, as well as stretching to the edges of his periphery, and he could make out vague forms in the dark mass: the outlines of buildings, and large industrial machines moving between them.

The preacher had halted because a thought had occurred to him. He was returning to the City to try and stop the others from becoming nothing again, but if he went back, he too would surely lose himself.

He didn't want that.

He didn't want that *because,* he corrected himself, if he was lost then he could not save the others. And there were droids still in the towns; those who could yet be convinced to stay, and those who had no intention to go but nevertheless needed his help.

The preacher looked back over his shoulder and drummed his fingers on his thigh, struggling with his thoughts. He stood like that for several minutes. Finally he shook his head and, uttering a laboured, grinding sigh, continued on to the City.

In time the sun dipped fully below the horizon, and the moonless night removed the desert and the City, leaving the droid in a pitch black gulf. He carried on regardless, secure with his internal compass, not needing it when his destination was directly in front of him and its borders stretched out further than he could have naturally deviated. During the day the preacher's mind had wandered; he had reminisced, or considered theology idly. Now, though, he ceased to think of anything at all, as if his thoughts came not from him, but from the light that had shone on him. He walked on mechanically.

After several miles something appeared in the distance that piqued the preacher's interest, rousing him from his benumbment. A green glowing dot, punctuating the empty sands. Faint at first, it grew brighter and larger as he moved towards it, until he could distinguish its shape: the number 436, etched in light on the nighttime darkness. As he came up to where the eldritch figure floated, he saw that it was a digital readout mounted on a wooden signpost. The glow from the diodes lit up the words written around it. They read:

Norton's Retreat
Population 436

Fourteen Miles West

As he looked at the sign the population figure turned from green to red, before switching off. It turned back on a moment later, green again, but now read 435. The preacher felt a tinge of sadness at this silent little death. At the same time it reminded him of his earlier dilemma. There were droids here that he was sure he could save.

Except . . .

He looked past the sign, in the direction of the City. Much of that argument made sense, he knew, but it was the feeling of relief that came with the idea that turned him against the it, and shamed him. Yet that relief was very compelling.

He worried with the arrow nailed to the post, twisting it around before conscientiously returning it to its original position. At last he moved past the sign, continuing on his path, but after a dozen steps he turned, heading in the direction his compass told him was west.

Behind him the counter flickered again, to read 434.

❀

The sun had been up for one hour and twenty-six minutes, according to the preacher's internal clock, when he arrived at Norton's Retreat. The archway he passed under — three wooden beams, roped together — no longer bore the name of the town, but the preacher knew it to be the right one, because he knew it to be the only one. As a long-time traveller he had a thorough knowledge of the desert, and before now had had no reason to assume that this present expanse was anything but empty.

Secluded, he thought, puzzling over the idea. It was true that the desert had been populated as droids had sought to escape, but they had been escaping from a life, not other droids. Loneliness could turn to senility so easily.

'So easily,' he muttered, unaware that he had spoken.

As he walked down the main street, his long-distance trudge now a more inquisitive stroll, he became quickly aware of the silence, the emptiness; there was no movement to be seen through the dark windows of the buildings he passed, no sounds to be heard inside.

The preacher frowned, ferrous dust sifting from his brow and onto his fading poncho. The sign had indicated a population of over four hundred: not a large number, but sizeable enough given the small town it belonged to. Yet, nothing.

To the left, in the distance, a thud made the droid's head swivel. Another thud followed a moment later, and with it came a more continuous sound; a low rumbling that he couldn't identify. The preacher quickened his pace, coming to a crossroads and turning off the main street.

He came to a stop as he saw them: the residents of Norton's Retreat. They were some way up the street, spilling out of the building they had been in, droid after droid. His mouth fell open in shock as he began to realise what they were doing — what they had been doing.

Then he smiled. They were coming out of the town's church — they had been at morning prayer.

It was an inspiring scene. Dozens of settlements he'd seen, maybe a hundred or more, and not in one of them had he ever seen a congregation this size. Memory of the silence elsewhere in town, and a quick depth scan and extrapolation, suggested that the entire population was there in front of him.

As the preacher walked up to the crowd he raised his hand in salute. Most of the droids were too far away or involved in their conversations to notice him, but several nearby turned in his direction. One, a short, stocky female, apparently appraising both the hand gesture he used and his attire, stepped forward.

'Preacher-man, right?' she said. She was direct, but her words were not spoken unkindly. He nodded confirmation at her.

'A blessing y'are then,' she responded, evidently relieved despite her gruff manner. 'As you can see, we try to keep the faith as best we can, but it ain't as it should be without one of His messengers to lead us.'

'You have no clergy?' This threw him. He had never seen such a large congregation before, not one even worth comparing to this, but the largest he had seen had always been led. It was the preacher's experience that without one of his kind, no more than a few droids in any town would remain religious.

She spotted the consternation on his face and placed a hand on his arm.

'Ain't the usual way o' doin' things, I know. Things're different round here lately; if you'll come back to my place, preacher-man, I'll explain it all for ya.'

✾

Her name was Camille, and her small house was sparsely decorated but comfortable. The preacher sat at her kitchen table as she moved around the room, accommodating her morning chores as she spoke to him.

'Oh, there were some of us went away,' she was saying, 'quite a number if I'm bein' truthful; maybe seventy or more. Some o' the businesses in town closed up a'cause o' that, either when folk stopped payin' them custom or when the owners left for the City themselves. Retreat started to get pretty quiet around then.

'I guess most of us would'a gone away, too. Certainly plenty more who're still here had been talkin' o' leaving. But a month or so after the first folk had started off for the City, a big electrical storm came down between here an' there, four or five miles out'a town. It turned back those who'd just started out, and one poor fellow, he even got caught up in it. Came back ravin' and delusional, an' died shortly after. Well, after we'd all seen him, none of us somehow had an urge to leave town anymore.

'An' this is how you've found us, preacher. Town might be less busy than it used to, but there's still work to be done an' folk to do it, and around that we find ways o' occupying our time.' She looked down at the rag she was dusting surfaces with and said, more quietly but with an honesty the preacher respected, 'I guess church-goin' might be somethin' we do for at least partly that reason.' She looked up at him. 'Still, it means that we go . . .'

'There are worse distractions,' he said.

'Ayuh.' She dropped her gaze as she said it, opened her mouth slightly as if to say something more, then closed it and looked back at him. 'Anyway, it sure is a blessin' that you're here, preacher. We're good, clean-livin' folk for the most part, but we have our troubles like anybody does, an' the words of one of His to guide us'd be mighty welcome. If you're willin' to offer that, o' course.'

He smiled at her politeness. It was a common convention that travelling preachers such as he would always stop for a little at any place they came to, and would always answer any reasonable request made of them: it was a sign of their faith, as well as character-istic of the sort of demeanor a droid had to have to take up this life. Nevertheless, droids who asked him for favours often became shy, even those who would stand up to tyrants. It had made the preacher wonder before if something of the Maker could be seen in His mes-sengers, though he always dismissed the thought as vanity.

Camille was looking at him with patience. Despite the caveat, the preacher had recognised the slyness about this droid: when she had first identified him, it was obvious that she expected him to lead a few sermons for them. The hospitality was not a sham, though. She was clever, but that did not preclude her from being a good droid, which she seemed clearly to be.

He nodded. 'I'll stay. For a while, at least.'

＊

Camille offered him her spare room for the night, saying with apolo-gies that he would have to find accommodation somewhere else in the town after a day or two, as 'folk've got a tendency to talk'.

He sat on the bed, which looked to have been freshly made that morning, though Camille had not known he would be arriving then; she clearly found comfort in routine. The droids of Norton's Retreat went to church every morning for a prayer and a reading, leaving the preacher little time to prepare a sermon. A first service was crucial, as if the first in a place went poorly it would often mean that the ones after, no matter how thought-provoking or inspirational, would not be properly heeded. If the first service went well, a congregation could be led by their preacher to do things they would never have expected of themselves.

At four minutes past midnight, the preacher decided that a walk would aid his thoughts, and stood up. As he did so, he heard movement outside his door; footsteps moving down the stairs, and the front door opening and then closing. Presuming Camille had had a similar idea to him, and mindful of her prophecy of gossip spreading, the preacher resolved to postpone his own walk until she had returned.

When that finally happened, the preacher had found inspiration for his piece — entitled 'The Courage for Sacrifice' — and spent the rest of the night instead sitting in quiet reflection.

✿

The corpses were so disfigured as to be barely identifiable.

The victims — three of them — had clearly suffered. Parts were scattered, bent and broken, everywhere. They had been torn out of the three droids whilst they had still lived: the ground around them was charred where sparks had flown from live circuitry.

Two of the dead droids lay in pieces on the sand; the third was tied haphazardly to a post, with rope around her legs and her neck. Her corpse was largely whole, but with the ability to recognise her as a once living thing the grotesque nature of her death was merely highlighted: she had been stripped naked, and her chest torn open, the metal bent backwards around her as she had been frantically disembowelled. On her battered face was a look of horror.

On the ground in front of her, a man was moaning wretchedly. It was the same man that had called at Camille's house that morning — she being his neighbour — saying that his wife was missing. They had gone with him to search for her, meeting a few more droids on the way who had noticed the absence of the other two, and before long had found this place, on the outskirts of town.

The preacher surveyed the unfortunate three quietly. He had witnessed death before, two or three times, but before it had not been so savage and senseless. The deaths he had seen before had been over a dispute; the murder had served simply as a solution to it. Here, however, the killer's apparent rage was overwhelming. The effort to mutilate so intensely was far greater than the effort it would have required to simply kill the three; the rest was clearly to satisfy some powerful anger. Or lust, the preacher imagined sourly.

Camille came to his side and placed her hand briefly on his arm. 'I wish you hadn't seen this,' she said.

'It isn't your fault.'

She dismissed his words, turning back to the corpses.

'No matter how many times you see tragedy, it always kicks you in the gut.' She sighed. 'If it had only been me instead . . . '

'Someone else would be mourning.'

She looked around at him, then dropped her eyes. 'Maybe so.' After a moment she breathed in deeply, then turned to the rest of the gathered droids and began directing them in clearing up the remains.

The preacher walked away. He would be asked to say words to see off the deceased later, but for now this was their time. They would thank him if he helped, of course, but in their hearts they would consider it an intrusion. Besides, he needed to leave them for a moment. His revulsion at the scene had temporarily overcome him, and he needed also to think. The incident was unsettling him in its gratuitousness: he failed to see what could lead a droid to kill — destroy, even — another in that manner. And the behaviour of the townsfolk troubled him. Each one of the group seemed resigned to the morbid discovery. The husband wept, but even he had displayed no surprise at his wife's death. They were sad, but not apparently shocked. It made the preacher wonder if this had happened before.

It was not the time now to question such things. Whatever the true nature of this incident, it was clear enough that they were aggrieved by it, and as a preacher it was his duty now to guide them, give them strength again. The subject of his sermon would need to change; last night's topic had become inappropriate, even callous, in this morning's dark light.

An object bounced off the preacher's boot as he walked and he stooped to pick it up. It was an eyeball, dangling between his finger on copper filaments.

Slightly repulsed, he turned to take it back to the group. He knew, at least, what his replacement topic would be.

✿

For such a small town, it was an unusually big church. The preacher counted fourteen rows of pews, and six more for the choir behind the pulpit he was standing at. It was not enough, though; droids were pressed tightly onto every seat and still some were forced to stand in the aisle. If there had been this attendance before the migration began, he reckoned, they would have been spilling out of the building.

A moment of inspiration took the preacher. If the people of this town had no intention of going to the City, there could be others doing the same elsewhere. He could turn this place into a spiritual haven — it essentially was already — and then . . .

It wasn't a spiritual haven. Not even a haven now; far from it. The preacher became sombre again. He turned to the pre-arranged hymn schedule and almost laughed bitterly, reading out the first: 'Welcome, Delightful Morn'.

The hymn ended, and for a few moments the preacher stood in silence. When he finally spoke, his voice was low.

'When I go to prepare a service,' he began, 'I like to wait a while first, and see what occurs around me in that time. I prefer not to choose a subject, but have it inspired naturally. It always comes more easily that way, and to me feels more relevant, for myself and for the congregation I am serving.'

He sighed. 'Today, I wish I had not had my inspiration.'

The preacher looked out over his audience, noting the faces that he recognised. Camille sat in the front row; he spotted other members of that morning's search party around the church. Only the husband of the woman who had been tied to the pole was not present, but it did not surprise the preacher that the man needed some time to grieve alone.

He looked back briefly to his quickly scrawled notes — short jottings of key thoughts he'd had — before continuing.

'As you are all by now aware, three of your number were lost this morning, before their time. Their names were Erin Lanning, Ethan Robertson and Karl Bergin, and from what I have been told it would seem that they were good, honest folk. I wish I could say that their passing was peaceful, but this was far from the case. A killer is in your midst.'

Their expressions largely remained neutral, but the preacher had expected no more; few of these droids had been built with moveable facial features and so were confined to the — mostly blank — expressions they had been designed with.

'My first thought when I witnessed the tragedy presented this morning was to talk of vengeance; of smiting the sinner thrice over for his every wrongdoing. When I felt calmer, I thought of speaking of repentance and forgiveness, and loving thy neighbour. But I came to realise that I need not be so formal. I can be more direct, and in this hour of sorrow I should be more direct.

'Because sitting here before me I see an entire town. You are all there is of Norton's Retreat, and Norton's Retreat is all there is in several miles of desert. If I am addressing all the droids there are to address, then I am addressing the killer. It sickens me to think so, that the droid responsible for the evil that occurred last night can attend a holy service without shame. Nevertheless, their presence means I may implore them to repent.

'I have seen droids fight each other, and harm each other, and even kill each other, on many occasions. Each time has been a most terrible sin. Not one of those times before have I ever seen evil to compare to the evil I saw this morning. But heed my warning: he who is responsible for this, without penance, will suffer in the next life pain and horror far worse than that his victims faced at his hand, and that torment shall last an eternity. Only if he turns back from the path of evil and begs forgiveness may he be spared his fate.'

All the while the preacher spoke he scanned the congregation. Most stared at him with their immobile expressions; one or two others had their heads lowered, lost in their own thoughts and troubles. When his eyes met Camille's she looked away from him, and an unsettling impression came to him, that there was guilt in her reaction. The preacher dismissed the notion for now; he would think on it later.

He sighed, quietly enough that his congregation would not hear him do so. He had said enough on the matter today, but it would remain a predominant theme yet in the sermons to come. For now, he turned to the passage he had selected to read. The subject was confession. Hymns would follow, and then he would say a little more on the deceased; a prologue to the funeral in the afternoon.

He was distracted from these thoughts though; even from the reading, despite its relevance. His mind continued to wander over the off-putting reactions of Retreat's droids to the deaths. It left him with the uncomfortable feeling that some of the townsfolk knew more than they chose to say. He could not shake the notion that the morning's tragedy was not isolated; there had been more deaths before now, and there would be more yet to come.

The sun was setting on the preacher's third day in Norton's Retreat. The morning had seen a further two victims, tied to each other by wiring torn from their throats. His sermon that day had beseeched the killer to reveal themselves, throw themselves on the town's mercy before it became so late that only vengeance could be considered.

The sermon had felt redundant. However strangely apathetic the townsfolk appeared to be, the preacher felt certain that it was already too late for mercy, and the killer surely knew that as well. Mostly, though, his words felt redundant because he had come to doubt that he needed the killer to come forward. The preacher thought he had probably already discovered the identity.

That previous night he had spent again in Camille's spare room. She had seemed reluctant to have him stay, citing her previous reasoning, but her neighbour's grief was too great for the preacher to retire there.

He had been sitting on the bed, thinking quietly over that day's events, when he had heard Camille pass his door and begin down the stairs. It was four minutes past midnight. Crossing to the window, the preacher looked down into the street and watched Camille as she left the house and walked away. Her gait was different: when he had previously seen her she moved with a relaxed confidence, now her strides were fast, and the pacing between steps was irregular, jittery.

Memories filled his mind. Her reaction at his mention of 'worse distractions'. Her dismissal of his claim that the first deaths had not been her fault. The way she had looked away from him during the sermon.

The preacher went back to the bed, sitting down on it awkwardly, clutching his head in his hands. He could not believe those thoughts; could not imagine Camille committing such crimes. He had seen no evidence of that capacity in her personality. Besides, he reasoned, why would a killer invite a stranger, a preacher no less, into their home? He struggled with the dilemma, whether to follow her, or to dismiss his paranoia and not break her trust in him, until he heard her return: after that, he laid staring at the ceiling, filled with dread.

When they found the bodies in the morning, they had been out of town in the same direction Camille had taken the night before.

So now, as the third night approached, the preacher crouched pensively behind a drinking trough on the side of the road opposite Camille's abode.

He had told her that afternoon that the events of the past days had disquieted him, and he had decided to spend the night in prayer, asking the Maker for guidance. He had worried that his nervousness would show, that Camille would realise she had been discovered, and at first she did seem concerned that he would not be staying in her house or another's. When he mentioned, however, that he would be confined to the church for the night, she became agreeable.

The preacher, as was his habit when approaching a confrontation, fiddled unconsciously with his left index finger. He unscrewed it a little way, then tightened it again; unscrewed it, tightened it. Rust trickled thinly from the gap as he did so.

At four minutes past midnight a shadow moved across one of the upper windows, and a moment later Camille appeared at the front door, pulling it open with the awkward, almost manic motion he had seen last night. She lurched two steps out into the road, then stopped, and turned to look directly at the preacher.

He became static, locking all his joints, not daring to move, and all the while meeting Camille's gaze. Diodes had activated in her eyes, lighting her face in alternating reds and oranges. His unscrewed finger fell from his grasp, hitting the sand with a quiet thud, and he looked in terror to see if those deranged eyes would follow the sound.

Eventually she turned, having apparently not seen him in the darkness, and staggered away, one arm swinging erratically. The preacher waited a short while, as much out of shock as caution, and then set off to follow her.

Her movements, which he continued to observe on their haphazard jaunt across Norton's Retreat, the preacher found to become more and more unsettling. They were so removed from the body language that he had previously experienced of Camille that she seemed almost to be another droid, or some alien entity. Moreover, the irregularity of her steps and the swinging lurch began to affect the preacher like some form of motion sickness; echoes of the unexpected pattern of footsteps made it sound as if there were others walking nearby. In the light of the passing street lamps the waving arm splayed lunging shadows on the walls. It worsened the delusion that there were other travellers around them, by causing the preacher to imagine that he saw them out of the corner of his eye as they passed side streets and alleyways.

This unnerving impression made him almost want them to reach Camille's destination sooner, were it not for his dread at the prospect. He was afraid. Afraid that he was about to see yet more innocent droids receive incomprehensible torment, afraid that, given Camille had apparently the strength to overcome groups of two and three droids and tear open steel, he would not be able to save her victims; he was afraid that not only would he not be able to stop her, but that she would turn on him as well. He was prepared for death, but terrified of the agony that could come before it.

Yet it was another fear that came closest to driving the preacher away from his pursuit. He was afraid that he would be proved correct: that Camille would be the killer. The preacher found that he really did not want this, would rather that the killer remained undiscovered. He found that he did not think he could cope with Camille's identity being subject to such incredible change: he abhorred the thought that a droid's personality could be lost like that.

He looked to the maddened figure in front, and thought it maybe too late to hope such a thing could not happen. That made him falter. For a few seconds he simply stood and watched as Camille loped away, but when she turned a corner he hurried after her, not knowing if he still wanted to follow her but knowing that if he waited now he would lose the choice.

Moving past the building Camille had just disappeared behind, the preacher realised with apprehension that they had reached the edge of town, which meant that the night's sojourn must almost be at an end. He began to tremble at the thought but continued anyway, following Camille up one of the dunes that enclosed this side of Norton's Retreat. They quickly crested it, revealing the view across the desert.

The sight made the preacher drop to his knees with a sob, his strength gone.

＊

He sat quietly in the church, watching the stained glass windows begin to glow as the sun rose. He could hear droids moving past outside. They would find the bodies soon, and though he knew they would need him then, he could not find the strength to join them. There seemed little point. These droids knew already what to expect, and the preacher didn't doubt that their expectations would continue to be met, morning after morning. There was a way, he believed, that the killer could be stopped, but before that could happen the townsfolk would need to have the nature of their enemy explained to them, and now was not the right time for that.

He thought back to the night's events, mere hours ago but already ancient in his mind and unforgettable. He had crested the dune, twenty yards behind Camille, and the first thing he knew was that he was correct. She was the killer. She wasn't alone though: the other droids he thought he had imagined seeing and hearing had actually been real. Most had arrived before he and Camille had gotten there, but some were still approaching, leaving the town from different routes, moving past and around the prostrate preacher, ignoring him as they headed to their destination.

The killers numbered every droid in town.

He had watched them, unbelieving, as they gathered together, all moving in that jerky, shambling way he had seen Camille behave. Their eyes all glowed, and their was no denying their corruption; they groped and tugged at one another, spinning each other around and leaping awkwardly about. It looked to the preacher like some brutal, degenerate waltz.

Yet he had been confused. There seemed to be no signs of violence, no victims amongst the droids in front of him: and if the entire town was present here, that left no possibility for there to be a victim. As he had thought this, several droids had lifted a wooden pole from the centre of the writhing crowd. Those near to it stopped their disturbing dance to help force the pole securely into the sand. This task achieved, one of their number climbed out of the mass, stepping up on the shoulders of others until he could reach the top of the pole. He clung to it, and stepped away from the crowd, to hang in the air. Other droids started to climb up too, but with different intent: they carried rope, and began tying the first droid in place. He howled as they did this, but the noise, bestial as it was, the preacher had to admit to himself could be nothing other than laughter.

The final knot was tied, and the townsfolk around the pole fell back a little, becoming silent and still. Those behind them followed, and peace travelled through the crowd until they all stood quietly, save only the bound droid, who continued his lunatic laughing.

As one the townsfolk descended on him, and the preacher watched stunned as they scrabbled over one another to tear at him, clawing at his legs, finding places to dig in with their fingers. The pole began to bend forward, but others grabbed at it, and at the bound droid's neck, holding it in place. Finally, his waist began to tear, and as it did so the bound droid became instantly lucid, the animal cackling replaced with screams; a natural sound that seemed out of place in that writhing nightmare. He struggled against his neighbours, flapping his hands in futility at the rope around his wrists. His screams doubled and trebled in volume as his legs were ripped away. Before they were lost in the orgy, the preacher saw several droids bite at them, including one whom he had seen share a hymn-book with the current victim at that morning's sermon.

The preacher moaned, but did not look away. The dying droid continued to writhe, but his movements were weaker and his screams had become moans. The townsfolk left him, turning in on themselves, and a moment later another droid was lifted over the heads of the crowd. Like the first victim, she too was laughing maniacally. They carried her to the pole and without pause thrust her head-first into the sparking bowels of the dismembered droid. Her laughter stopped, and she began to spasm violently as she was electrocuted in the torn circuitry of her mutilated neighbour. Smoke poured from her and she exploded, showering herself over the crowd. Large components collided with two of the townsfolk, damaging them, and the rest turned now on these two, clawing and biting, frenziedly pulling them apart, any semblance of purpose they may have had now gone.

At this point the preacher had walked away, setting off back to town, heading to the church. He had stayed there for the remaining hours of the night. Eventually he heard the townsfolk coming back; their footsteps still sounded uneven, but seemed calmer, as if the murder had lifted them of a burden. After a while the sound of the droids died away, and when they returned they were in smaller groups and moved regularly again.

They would find the bodies soon. When they did, the preacher knew that their emotions would be genuine. Whether they remembered what they'd done, or forgotten it on waking, they would nevertheless be distraught, and they would mourn, and they would damn the killers, even though the killers were themselves. The preacher understood this, because he had recognised the underlying motivation of the night's events.

The church doors opened. The preacher didn't turn, but waited until Camille came and sat beside him. In silence they stared at the front window, where sunlight was now shafting through in brilliant rays.

Eventually Camille spoke.

'Thought I'd find y'here,' she said quietly. The preacher didn't respond, and they both remained facing forward.

'I saw you last night,' she continued. 'When I left to... when I left the house. An' I guess you saw that I saw you, but I suppose you probably didn't know if I was actually seein' anythin' or not at that time. But I remember seein' you now, and at the time I think I probably knew I was seein' ya. Didn't matter much though. When we . . . in that state we get in, only thing matters is those ones we're . . . ' Her voice broke, but she composed herself, finishing bravely, 'Only thing matters is those we've chosen to kill.'

She turned to him. 'Guess you saw that, too. No reason you'd've been hidin' if you weren't following me, and no reason you'd still be here if you didn't have somethin' big on your mind,' she said. She wasn't being accusatory, but she also showed no fear of recrimination. She was confessing to him.

Concentrating on her hands, clasped and resting in her lap, she explained. 'Don't know how it happened, but we weren't always this way. Time was there was almost no crime in this town. We've got good folk here, or had. Then all of a sudden one night, everyone takes off to the desert, and we murder a few of our own. Started not long after we gave up on goin' to the City. I've often wondered if that had somethin' to do with it, like it's cabin fever of sorts, but it just comes on too strong to be a simple thing like that.

'Anyway, after the first time, when we realised what we'd done, we all hurried to church and prayed. I've never seen so many folk be so openly humble like that. We begged the Maker for forgiveness, and vowed such a thing would never happen again.

'O' course, it did, and each time after we prayed not only to be forgiven but also for the strength to stop what we were doing. He never gave us that strength, but when you came I thought . . . '

Camille stopped, sighed raggedly, and closed her eyes. The preacher waited with patience.

'I thought,' she said slowly, 'that with you we might've been able to stop this . . . evil. We haven't, and I don't think we ever shall.'

Suddenly she turned to him, eyes looking imploringly into his. 'We don't mean to do it,' she said, desperation straining her voice.

'When it happens, it's like we're dreamin'. You see what's going on, you feel like you mean to do whatever you do, but really you aren't in control. It's only in the morning that we're ourselves again, and not one droid in this town has woken up thinkin' that they did the right thing the night before. We hate it, but we do it again an' again, killin' our friends an' our families; whoever it feels right to kill. We don't know what to do, preacher, and we've tried, but we just don't know what's wrong with us!'

As she said this, she had gripped one of the preacher's hands in hers, and now he placed his free hand on them. Very slowly, he said, 'I do.'

❁

The preacher looked out across the congregation, who sat in sombre silence, and explained to them what he had told Camille half an hour previously.

'You have a virus,' he said. 'It has corrupted your system; it is what makes you kill each night. I have, on my travels, seen such things before, though I confess to never having seen a sickness of this magnitude.

'I cannot say for certain how it was contracted, but I believe it came first to your droid who suffered in the electrical storm. The cause is, however, no longer important. The virus is no longer infectious; this can be seen in that I remain free of it. The only concern now is to cure it. Prayer, alas, can do you no good. This virus is not His work, but rather comes from below. Nor will you find a mechanical cure, for this virus infests the furthest depths of your circuitry.

'Before the migration, in towns less isolated than Norton's Retreat, I saw viruses being removed. The method agreed upon was to transfer it out of the victim, and into a small, inanimate device. The virus was not destroyed in this way, but it was rendered harmless. There is not this technology available to us, and I do not understand it well enough to replicate it. Even should I be able to, this infection is too large, I should think, to be contained in such an artifact. However, I think there may be another solution. It is not ideal, and does not make the virus entirely safe, but it will spare all of you who remain in this town from its effects.'

The preacher paused, reluctant. Breathing in, he stiffly made his proposal.

'I will take the virus into myself, and exile myself from any population.'

The congregation broke into murmured discussion. None, the preacher noted, made any protest at his suggestion.

One droid spoke up.

'Will it work?'

'I'm not sure,' the preacher answered, 'but it should. If you are worried about the containment capacity needed I can tell you that a virus, whilst deeply rooted, is small; I could take it in many times over without being affected much more significantly.'

They fell back to their conversation, and he left them to it. In time they all became silent again, looking at the preacher tentatively. It was that old politeness; they knew what they wanted, and knew that the preacher would be compelled to provide it. To ask for it, however, would be rude.

The preacher closed his eyes and said, his voice wavering, 'I will do this for you.'

✹

Night drew in, and the preacher stood on the edge of town, waiting. The townsfolk of Norton's Retreat did not know in advance where their fevered ritual would take place, but they had noticed a regular pattern to the choice of location on any particular night, and so could direct him to the approximate area. Sure enough, at seventeen minutes to midnight, the first droid came shambling into view, her eyes glowing.

At the sight of her the preacher shuddered.

His decision here was inescapably costly, possibly worse than going back to the City. There, more of what he was would be lost, but at least he would be less aware of what had gone. With the virus, he would wake up each morning to remember just how he had changed; to know the monstrous being he had become. Contrarily, the risk in going to the City was that he would sacrifice his identity without saving other droids. Here, he would certainly be freeing others, and was likely to retain at least a part of himself.

More of the townsfolk were coming into view now, going over to begin their groping, cumbersome dance with the first one.

There was, though, still the risk that he was wrong; the virus might consume him entirely. If that were to happen, it could make the virus more dangerous. Here it was contained amongst the townsfolk, but it was in the preacher's nature to travel. If his mind was gone, he would not refrain from going to other towns, and bringing destruction on the droids there. Worse, he might not be able to remove the virus all of from the townsfolk. If it remained in some of them, Norton's Retreat would continue to see tragedy.

At least three hundred droids were gathered in front of the preacher, contorting gracelessly. It was four minutes past midnight; Camille would be setting off to join their number. It was almost time.

If he was lost to the virus, and brought it to others in other towns, a few droids might die before he was subdued. If he wasn't capable of removing it entirely from the townsfolk here, some more of them might die before they realised and were forced to destroy the remaining infected ones. Either of these things would be a tragedy.

If he did not attempt to remove the virus, four-hundred and twenty-five droids would certainly die.

In the crowd before him, two wooden poles were being raised up.

Panic rushed through the preacher. He did not want to lose himself, did not want to shamble around each night a monster. Death was one thing, a brief thing; a droid passed through it quickly and moved on. This virus, however, incurable because of its size and the migration, was something else. Something potentially eternal.

A droid had climbed the poles and was hanging between them, a hand and foot tied to each. The droids beneath were clutching at her indiscreetly, whilst she laughed that unsettling laughter.

He was a preacher. His function was to save other droids from sin and misfortune, at cost to himself if necessary. This situation defined that function. That function was only something he had chosen for himself.

The droids at the centre of the crowd had become silent.

They would curse him. Camille, and maybe one or two others, would understand his reasoning, but most of the townsfolk would curse him. Eventually even those trying to forgive him would come to damn his name. He would be a hated figure in Norton's Retreat; his name would be uttered bitterly on the final breath of the last droid to die of the virus. He would curse himself, too. He would live on with the memory of this deed, and torment himself to his end thinking of it. Yet he would also be able to find others to save this way. Others he could save.

He smirked bitterly at his own defence.

With a last look at the quietened crowd, the preacher shook his head and turned away from Norton's Retreat, walking off as the laughter turned to screams.

Top Night Out

JON GARRAD

WHITE CROW LIES INDOLENT AT THE DYING END OF ANOTHER DAY. In the topmost suite of an empty hotel Balfour looks down at what his father called a town and his grandfather called a city and knows for a fact he looks upon a tomb. His eyes wander up and down the single main street, searching for something new, something to relieve the endless staring.

Nothing. Theodore Brown of Brown's Crafts and Repairs stands in his empty doorway, a bottle in his hand and a knowing nonchalance about his crooked limbs, waiting for custom that never comes. Across the street his daughter Dora lurks behind her shutters, waiting for nightfall, waiting for freedom. They never speak. Balfour knows, or thinks he knows, what transpired between them in his father's day, and never speaks of it himself.

The saloon named for the town is silent. Balfour's tired, world-weary eye of the mind pictures Silas and Will hunched over the draughts board, studying the battlefield, plotting grand strategies that never come to pass in a game that never really seems to start. Occasionally one of them moves a piece, shuffling it across the board or picking it up and laying it down with an empty hollow click.

The church stands emptier than the saloon, its windows broken or boarded shut. Inside, at the foot of the altar, Father Whitman lies in pieces, the victim of his own despair. The padre may still be functional. Balfour wouldn't know: he hasn't set foot in the church for years.

A door swings open, further down the street, and Balfour's eyes automatically flick away from the deserted church to watch Doll lurch out. She does this every day, comes clattering out to lounge in the saloon making eyes at anyone who looks her way. She spends a lot of time staring into space. Balfour wonders, as he's often wondered, if anyone's ever fallen in love with her.

White Crow Street forks around the church. From there out to the mine, the town is nothing but residences, tin shacks thrown up to give droids some way to tell their own space from other people's. It was a largely meaningless gesture once, given the time they all spent together, but now it's given them somewhere to throw themselves down and reflect on what used to be the future.

Balfour's gaze is drawn up the left fork, which rises toward the hills, toward the mine. He dares not look too high. If he stares down the sunset, Balfour will look upon the broken, dusty heart of White Crow, and he has no need to see that again. Wheels that no longer turn, chains that hang still in baking, dusty air, tools resting where they fell decades ago . . . tools that carved the letters on the roofs of the houses of White Crow, the houses that have become gravestones over dead lives and deader secrets.

No. Balfour dares not look that way. He turns a little in the window, turns his back on the sunset, and looks downhill toward the schoolhouse. Here, at least, is life. Of a sort. There is nothing left for the children of White Crow to learn other than the one lesson the town itself can teach them: that their lives are over before they've really started. To them, though, this is vindication. Children, Balfour reflects, don't need a reason for anything, don't worry about purpose and lost hope. Or do they? Are those tiny running figures in the distance nagged by the thought that one day they'll have to stop playing . . . and what then?

Nagging doubts are common currency in White Crow. The children are tumbling through the gates, going home to empty houses and faces that would fix a smile if they could. They must know. They must have caught a hint by now. Balfour stamps that thought out, turns from the window. At least their families can fake smiles.

As he walks away, there's a flash of light on the windowpane. Something new. Something unexpected. Balfour rushes to the window and looks up the road toward the schoolhouse. The children are gathered round a clutter of brightly coloured vehicles. Engines gutter as they slow to idling: droids lean out, strange and wild droids painted in vivid quarter patterns and chaotic swirls, droids with smiles painted on to faces built without expressions. The schoolmistress runs from the building, drawn to cries and commotion. Her charges cluster around her. She holds up her hands for peace, steps between them, confers hastily with a rusted figure leaning from the foremost cab, and steps around behind the vehicle, out of Balfour's sight. Balfour watches, entranced, and sure enough, in minutes the caravan is turning in, fanning out across the schoolyard. The children are running home, running and laughing and smiling more than ever.

The carnival has come to town.

I first walked into White Crow along the mine road, coming into town from the west with the sun behind me. White Crow was a long way from anyplace I might be recognised, taken for something more than my mission. Long way from any place at all. Always struck me as funny how many droids came out to little towns like these to scratch a living under this devil of a sun, a long way from anyplace, a long way from guidance. That's my mission. Guidance. Keeping folk on the right road.

I walked into White Crow with this mission in mind, and as I walked down the one main street that hooked around the church I realised I'd have a hard time of it. I could see the carnival lights from the church wall where I stopped to rest, hear the oaths and cusses of the carnies and the grinding of gears. I hate that sound of filthy functions only just functioning at all; it's everything about sin and neglect and bad living condensed into a simple thing that means too much and sets me right on edge.

I'd have a struggle in White Crow all right. Carnival in town, and church not more than dust and superstructure. I stepped up and beat on the door. No answer came. I beat on the door again, harder.

'You won't get no answer there.'

I spun, faster than I'd moved in days, and saw a girl-child standing at the end of the path, ten feet or so away. She was a lash-up,
like most of the droids built in the desert, not much more than
spare parts, but she was smiling. All the children out here are built
with faces fair to break a power supply, 'specially if you're without one, and 'specially if they're standing in a gateway looking up
like you're some kind of angel. I took a few steps and knelt, close
to eye-level as I could.

'Why's that?'

'No pastor there to answer, sir, not since Father Whitman went
to pieces.' Her smile crept further out, and something told me she
wasn't being figurative.

'Can you tell me who's in charge round these parts?'

'Ain't no-one in charge, sir. Mister Balfour don't come out no
more, Mister Brown don't do business no more.'

'I see. And where might I find these fine gentlemen?'

'Mister Balfour's is right up the street,' she said, pointing at the
building facing down the church at the other end. Not what I'd call
pretty; crumbling stone and pillars, a pleasure palace falling down,
and drawn curtains in every window. I could barely even read the
sign. 'And Mister Brown's is just across there.'

'His blessings go with you, child.'

✱

The preacher is making Balfour nervous. He's young, but like an
older model in his lack of any facial features. Instead, there's just
the mirror-disc of his sensory apparatus, staring Balfour down with
his own distorted reflection. The preacher is wrapped up in black,
and has a wide-brimmed hat — compensating, perhaps, for a failed
circuit somewhere in his visual receptors. He trails dust.

'I appreciate all you're trying to do for us,' Balfour finally man-
ages to say, 'I really do. Ever since Father Whitman broke down
we've had nobody to minister to us. Doesn't make us beggars,
though. There's . . . there's folk in town as might not choose to be
ministered by a droid of your conviction.'

'My conviction, sir, is the conviction shared by all those who labour under His authority; by all created things. If there are droids among you who've forgotten that case of affairs — droids who I bear no ill will toward, since they've gone without a preacher so long — then it's my duty to remind them of it, and theirs to see that they should want reminding.' His voice is low and dry and cold, cold as a desert night, and he paces back and forth in a little cloud of dust as he speaks. 'The choice is not ours to make. He leads me where I might be of use, and it's clear to me that I'm of best use here in White Crow. 'He works in mysterious ways, His wonders to unfold.'

'That's as may be, father, but all I'm saying is that faith and duty ain't so much what we need right now. I know scripture says there's a bad fate in store for them as don't believe, but there's plenty of us think there's no fate worse than being stuck in White Crow.'

'Then I think I've got a topic for my first sermon.' The preacher stops his pacing and turns to face Balfour. Diodes flicker in the hotelier's face, and it takes an effort of will for him to face himself turned gargoyle in the preacher's dusty silver mask. 'Seems like there's a lot of you who could use an object example from a wandering man.'

✢

I stepped from the hotel feeling like my good works had already started. Richard Balfour had been a problem, it had to be said; a moral coward, shut up in his proverbial tower and looking out on a world he didn't have the gears to move in. To his credit, he'd come round fast enough, offering a room until such time as the church was made fitting. He hadn't seen fit to tell me precisely what had become of their Father Whitman, and I'd decided it was up to me to break open that church door and find out. I'd need tools.

Brown's Crafts and Repairs wasn't quite what I'd expected. A droid who makes it his business to keep his fellows in function ought to be able to manage himself, but T. H. Brown was obviously not of the same opinion; he'd been well-built once, but he was running to disrepair, showing wires and possessed of a leering look about his odd-sized optical receptors. Oil trickled down his leg, and there was a stink of cheap methylated coolant about him.

'You're Brown?' I tried to hide my contempt.

'Theodore of that set,' he growled, looking me up and down. 'So what can I do for you, preacher man?'

'I need tools and cleaning supplies. You've let your church get into quite some state.'

'Well,' said Brown lurching away from me, disappearing among the clutter of racks and disassembled machinery, 'that's pretty much White Crow all over. You come in by the mine?'

'I did. Leastaways, those ruins looked like a mine.'

'Them's the ones. White Crow wouldn't've been raised without those mines, an' she's fallin' down without 'em.' Brown emerged, laying a crowbar down in front of me. 'You want my advice, preacher, you'll let it do just that. Call it the Maker's will if it makes you feel better.'

'You want my advice, sir, you'll think twice before you take His name in vain or endeavour to sway His servants from their duty.'

'Damn, but you sound like old Whitman.' Brown tilted his head to one side with a hiss of loose hydraulics. 'He used to talk like that an' he was the first to crack. He prayed and prayed and prayed when the mine first started to fail. Got him down on his knees and begged deliverance. Later on he said it was divine judgement the mine failed, that we were all some kind o' sinners, and he stayed down and begged forgiveness. Know what happened then?'

'What happened then?' I leant in closer, staring him down, keeping my voice level.

'No deliverance, preacher man, an' no forgiveness. He prayed till he could hardly speak nor stand no more an' still no answer, an' finally he gave up prayin' for us at all. Last words we ever heard from him were condemnation. Last prayer he sent up was for the Maker to strike us all dead for our sins and save him from the futility o' his mission.' Brown didn't have lips to smile with, but if he had I was sure he'd have been grinning. He set down the bottle of industrial cleanser on the desk between us, nodded, and winked his oversized optic. 'Consider it my tithe, preacher man. 'Tain't like I'm in any place to worry over business.'

✻

The preacher walks away from Brown's Crafts and Repairs, down White Crow Street towards the church and the tumescent bustle of the carnival. Dora Brown watches him from behind her shutters, visual circuits sparking into unaccustomed effort, and she puts her hands together and offers up a prayer for the return of righteousness to White Crow. She sputters into movement, lurching up in a cascade of dust, and makes for the single cracked and spotted mirror. Tonight, she decides, will be a night to remember.

Three doors down on the far side of the street, Doll sits behind her veiled curtains with one hand trailing between her legs and lays her cheek on the other and sighs at the very sight of him. Behind her, a hand stirs amongst the covers, and she lies down with a deeper sigh, feels the grip bite down, mechanical pressure on the tense steel of her side, and she sighs again and dreams of love.

Silas and Will stare at the draughts board, neither willing to ever give ground and make a move. The barkeep looks up to watch the preacher pass and wonders idly if he's headed for the carnival. Silas pushes a piece across the board with a scraping sound.

The preacher steps up to the church doors. 'Let there be light,' he says with a smile, and drives the crowbar home.

✼

I decided to make my stand outside the schoolhouse gate that evening. Talking to Brown and finding Whitman had rattled me something terrible; White Crow needed help, that was for sure, and it would take all the devotion I could muster to give it. One thing I did know was that there could be no distractions. The carnival was my idea of a distraction. Folk losing themselves, convincing themselves that running from the truth could stand in the place of salvation. So I stood outside and made my stand, reaching out to everyone who passed my way, begged them to turn around and spend the night in wholesome prayer.

Some of them laughed. Most just walked by me, threw me off, ignored me. Children skipped by without a glance. Brown lurched through the crowd, sparing me a lecherous wink. More and more droids walked by, until there was nobody outside the gates but me.

I sighed, made the Maker's Mark over my head and followed the last of them in, trailing among the bright lights and booming sounds. Most of the crowd were heading for the biggest tent, thrown up more or less in the centre of the schoolyard, and I followed them through, regretting for once that I didn't have a face to set into to a scowl.

Inside . . . inside, I saw some horrible things. I had been expecting debauchery, carnival frenzy and wild abandon, but I had never dreamed it would be of such a vile sort as this. When first I walked in the lights were just coming up, strobing beams of bright colour into the dusty roped-off centre. Braziers flickered around and about, and a trapeze hung over my head.

There was a long moment of silence, and then the carnival droids rolled in.

Never in all my years have I laid eyes on such a cavalcade of monsters as I did that night. Droids with no legs pushing themselves forwards on wheels, droids with four legs, droids with three. Droids trailing sparks and wires from twisted bodies and open rents and tears. Droids with the most crude and horrid facial modifications imaginable, torn metal pushed through metal from the inside and spiking out like horrors from below.

They crept around the edge of their arena, thrusting themselves into the crowd, flaunting their deformities, rolling back and flashing exposed curves, cavorting under the lights and the streams of smoke pumping in from somewhere among the crowds. Not a word was spoken, not a note of music played; they just crept and touched and turned and twisted. I balled up my fists and begged the Maker for the strength I'd need to see this through, but as I prayed an amplified voice shook my thoughts away.

He'd stalked out of nowhere, tall and lean and wild, a droid dressed up and painted and carrying himself like he was the Maker Himself. He wore a long red coat and a tall black hat and he carried a cane with a mike at the top and he turned around to the audience and bowed.

'Ladies and gentlemen, children of all ages . . . welcome to the show.'

I swear I'm not a stranger to violence or to pain. I'm a droid of the world and I've suffered with the best of 'em, but that night I felt my diodes curling at every horror that fiend threw out at me. I saw droids lying across the fire, metal twisting, components crackling, and I heard them laugh like it was rapture itself to be there. I saw one giant droid bring down his hammer on a wreck of a cripple who rolled around and around with the giant's hat in his hand. The giant smashed him into spare parts, and I heard the folk of White Crow roar with laughter at the sight of it. I saw girl-droids writhing together in the flickering light of the strobes, and I could just picture every man in the room leaning in with his hand on his dynamo. The two of them picked each other open and wound their components round each other until you'd have sworn they'd been built as one. Droids with saws swung back and forth, lashing at the giant who'd broken up the dwarf and grinding off layers his outer casing in triumphant showers of sparks while two more dwarfs loaded a cannon, took careful aim and shot him down where he stood.

What made my system burn with fury, though, what made me want to rain down the Maker's wrath on White Crow and every citizen in it, was the way that demon ringmaster danced and stalked and cackled through it all, drawing the crowd on. Twice I met his gaze and twice I did not flinch and twice he looked away from me and roared with laughter. Twice I knew I had found my Enemy.

The lights flickered out, and I heard his voice.

'Thank you, ladies and gentlemen, and goodnight.'

The preacher stands in silent fury as the crowds throng out into the schoolyard. Droid carnies stand ready with games and treats and all the fun of the fair, grinning and leering under flickering electric lights. Balfour has a shotgun in his hands and is shooting parts off a dancing droid's head for prizes. Theodore Brown loiters round the fortune-teller's tent, deep in conversation with a curvaceous girl droid as dark as sin, his diodes crackling with anticipation. Doll has every free limb wrapped around the giant, her fingers toying with his scars. She kisses the dents in his chest and smiles. The children scamper from stall to stall, attraction to attraction, drawn in by beckoning fingers and dashing away with glee to the next distraction.

Outside the schoolyard, Dora Brown watches with disapproving eyes.

✸

'Hey. Preacher man.'

I looked up, fists still clenched, circuitry still blazing with rage. The ringmaster stood at the edge of the ring, watching me, head tilted on one side. He'd discarded the hat and traded the coat in for something a trifle less flamboyant, but there was that same sense of the strut and preen about him, even now, long after he'd stopped moving.

'You look smaller without your hat.'

Diodes flashed on and off in his eyes, approximating a smile. I realised then that his voice came from a grille in his mouth, not from anything that even approximated lips. The ringmaster was an old design. Very, very old.

'You can leave, y'know. Show's over. Run along.'

'We need to talk.'

'Do we now?' The ringmaster stepped over the rope and stalked toward me; was it my imagination, or were his legs jointed backwards? 'And what, pray, would an upstanding member of society such as you have to discuss with such a reprobate as I?'

'Just that. Keeping society upstanding.'

'Go on.' He halted a foot or so from me — uncomfortably close — and looked down at me, unflinching.

'Don't try to intimidate me, sir. Mine is a righteous course.'

'What business is that of mine?'

'You're impeding me in my course.'

'Oh.' He relaxed, hunched down a little, and rattled something behind his grille. 'And here was me thinking it was something serious.'

'There is nothing more serious than—'

'Than hellfire and damnation and loyal service to the Maker to avoid the previously described phenomena, am I right?' He half-turned, making to leave, but I caught him by the shoulder and turned him round to shout him down.

'Than every droid's duty to Him and to His Truth, sir! Your abomination and those like it have torn these folk away from the one path that can save them!'

'Padre, crank up your audio receptors and listen. You hear what's going on outside? It's laughter. Now from the state of you that's something that's not been heard in this town for quite a while, and you know what? You were here first.'

'I arrived at the same time you did.'

'Then you had the dying day to make these people see your truth. Night-time belongs to me and mine, padre. It's your doctrine that tells it so. I've had this argument back and forth with the likes of you more times than you've said sermons. Truth of it is there's never been a town that hasn't smiled a little stronger after we've rolled on, and plenty that's wept to lay eyes on the likes of you.' He swept my hand from his shoulder and laid his own on mine. 'Now I'm sorry my little show wasn't to your liking. I can quite see that. I can also see there's a truth to what you're saying. This is a poor town, and likely to see itself poorer if folk don't knuckle down and get to labour. That's not going to happen while we're still here to offer a . . . distraction.'

'You'll leave, then.'

'We'll be gone by tomorrow.' He held out his other hand, and with due reluctance I extended my own and shook. 'Peace on earth, padre, and goodwill to all.'

✿

I left my conference with the ringmaster filled with doubt. I'd heard the argument before, but as I walked out into the haze and shimmer of White Crow schoolyard I confess I felt I had done an evil thing. There were droids here laughing and cheering, where sunset had seen only silent, empty misery. There was joy here, no matter how tainted or misguided the source. I had been able to offer only censure. I had not inspired these folk.

I walked through the crowds with my hat turned down and collar turned up, addressing nobody, answering nobody. Children scampered across my path and I swerved to avoid them or stopped to let them by, not daring to face any of them.

The gates were open, and I walked back onto White Crow Street with my head hung low. As I passed by the church, though, I looked up to see two droids standing just inside the gate. One was the bolted-up girl-child, the first droid I'd spoken to in White Crow. The other . . . the other was a vision. She shone silver, bounced the carnival lights back in a wash of colours. She wore a long old-fashioned dress of a kind I'd not seen for years, and a veil hung down over her face. Not only that, but as I stepped closer I could see the Maker's Mark hanging round her neck, chains hooked into her hinges. It was golden.

Her hand rested on the girl-child's shoulder, and the girl smiled as she saw me. I bowed my head and made the Mark myself.

'You tried, Father,' she said to me eventually. Her voice crackled with long silence; I had the distinct feeling she'd spoken not a word in years. 'This town is raddled with sin. I know it. I know it better than most. You can save them, though. They haven't always been this way. One or two are rotten to the core; not functional. The others, though . . . ' and here she looked down at the girl by her side, 'the others have some good in them.'

'I . . . thank you, ma'am.'

'Dora. Miss Theodora Brown.'

'Father Ezekiel. Would you be . . . '

'Named for my father.' She looked away, awkward suddenly.

'And I for mine. Ministry runs in my family.'

'Apostasy, most fortunately, does not run in mine.'

'Fortunately indeed.' I bowed. 'I'll take my leave, if I may. The poor soul in the church . . . '

'I understand.' She stepped aside, and I passed under the archway toward the church. 'Father Ezekiel?'

'Yes?'

'Tomorrow's Sabbath.'

'I know. Service will be performed as is proper.' I heard her gasp, heard the rustle of cloth and the squeak of metal as she clasped her hands. 'You'll hear church bells tomorrow, Miss Dora Brown, and the Sabbath next, and the next, and every Sabbath until White Crow is saved.' I swear it in His name, and in yours and mine, and in all of ours. Tonight belongs to the carnival. Tomorrow belongs to me.

I cleared away the ruination of Father Whitman that night; laid him out and sent him on with my own hands, interring him in the ground behind the vestry wall, and I felt like singing as I did so. There was one good soul in White Crow, at least, and I would make sure that every last droid in town knew that there was still goodness among them, that there was still a chance for them to be saved.

Before I retired, I looked downhill toward the schoolyard, where the carnival lights had long shut down. 'Yes,' I said to myself. 'Tomorrow belongs to me.'

❇

The sun rises over White Crow, and it rises on tragedy. Richard Balfour throws open his doors with a new vigour, a new sense of excitement, and watches in horror as droids dash to and fro, weeping and crying and brandishing fists. He strides down the main street, intent on doing his duty as elder for the first time in many a year, and seizes the first droid he finds by the shoulder.

'What madness is this?'

'My daughter, sir! My daughter's gone!'

'Mine too!'

'My son . . . ran off in the night . . . '

'My sister . . . '

'My brother . . . '

Piece by piece, Balfour puts the story together. In every home that bore a child, save one, the child is gone. Some have disappeared. Some, though, have left explanations, scrawled notes of apology.

They have run away to join the circus.

Balfour's gaze flickers east to west, taking in the desolate mine that pinned down all their hopes, and the schoolyard, empty now but for the tracks of vehicles, scattered papers and spent shells, spilt coals and ash. Can he blame the children? Would he have stayed so long if he were a young droid with forever ahead of him? He draws in a deep breath, turns to face the crowds, and just as he's about to open his mouth and speak the church bell starts to ring.

❋

The droids of White Crow throng into the church. Dora Brown is waiting for them at the gate, out in the open and proud as she can be on such a day. Her daughter — the daughter they have long known she constructed — waits beside her. Sometimes she is greeted with foul looks, sometimes with fair. Some say she is here to preach over their grief, to remind them that the righteous and repentant Dora Brown has retained her child. Some rejoice that some good has come of this foulest of Sabbaths, that she is among them again, that one child at least has remained. All of them at least acknowledge her, and beneath her polished shell her circuits glow with pride.

Some faces are conspicuous by their absence; Balfour has passed Theodore Brown, leaning in his door and spitting coolant at the feet of passes-by, and Doll is nowhere to be seen. Some, like Dora, are conspicuous by their presence; nobody can remember the last time Will and Silas left their board for any cause or purpose. Balfour takes his place in the foremost pew, and watches as the preacher Ezekiel takes his place.

'Droids of White Crow. Brothers and sisters. Fellow children of the Maker. I have heard your cries this day, as I rose to sound the call back to righteous ways, and I have heeded them. You have lost your own children, those you crafted in homage to He who crafted you. They have left you, left their homes and their duties for evil ways.

'You heard me,' he continues as the murmurs begin. 'I spoke of evil, and I meant to speak of evil. I too was lenient, though you may not think it to hear me now. I too extended my tolerance to these vipers, for I too rejoiced to hear your children laugh. I thought that there must be some good in the vile and degenerate ways of these carnival folk if they could bring laughter back to the folk of White Crow.

'I was wrong. But I will not be wrong again. Where there was weakness, let there be strength. Where there was tolerance, misguided tolerance, let there be vengeance! The devils who have led your children from you are out there, in the desert! They leave tracks, and they can be followed! I say we march into that desert, united in His cause, and take back the children of White Crow!'

✱

I left the church — my church, I was beginning to feel — at the head of a mob. Balfour had been the first to stand and cheer, and others had followed. Now they fanned out across town, taking up what weapons they could find. Mister Brown had been quick to hide his disgust and set up shop, handing out heavy tools and flammable fluids, accepting any favour offered to him in return for the means to take back the children. I waited for them at the gate, my hat tilted back a little to let the sun fall on me. Miss Dora Brown waited at my side, her daughter clutched tight to her, her veil drawn down as close as ever.

'Something's worrying you,' I said to her as the populace went about their work. There was a silence.

'It's you,' she finally said. 'When you arrived, I thought . . . I thought you would bring hope.'

'I am restoring hope.' I turned to face her. 'These droids have lost their children; the only things of worth they've created in this town. They need them back.'

'Is it your place to lead them?' she hissed. 'Is it your place to spur them on to vengeance in the name of He who made them?'

'I — I don't know, Dora. I think they needed to be roused, somehow. This punishment from Him — what else could it be? This punishment for their indolence, this has roused them, but someone has to guide them. Balfour's elder of this town and he has no idea how to lead, and who then? Someone like your father?'

'No.' She was visibly shaken; I swear I heard sobs from beneath her veil. 'No, I see that. I just... I fear this is unholy work, Ezekiel. The work of destruction, not creation.' She looked down. 'I'm sorry.'

I closed my arms around her, hesitantly at first, and then held her tighter. 'Your tears will temper this day's acts, Dora.' I let her go, lifted her veil so I could look her in the optics. 'At sunset, we will bring the children back, and there'll be peace. I promise. I swear it. But until then, I bring not peace, but the sword. You have to understand that.'

'I understand.'

✻

We spilled out of White Crow, following the carnival's trail. It wasn't hard; their vehicles were old and left oil spattered among the tracks. Balfour walked alongside me, fidgeting with the length of iron in his hands; I didn't begrudge him his place at the head of the line. It was his duty as elder to be there, and it was about time he did it. I carried no weapon. It was their duty to exact vengeance, mine to guide it. It was their children who were at risk, not mine.

Before noon, I picked out the roar of engines ahead. Balfour and I had made our plans — or rather I had made them and he'd agreed. He would lead half the townsfolk left, I would lead the others right. No word would be spoken by anyone until we'd surrounded the troupe and I'd met Balfour ahead of them. This would be a show of strength, but silent; we'd make it clear we were all against them. After that, he was to leave the talking to me.

We broke left and right across the desert, picking our way across the baking ground. The vehicles slowed to a crawl, and the carnies poked out their heads to watch the townsfolk advancing. The giant leapt down from his place at the wheel of the largest wagon, taking up an iron the size of my arm, but the ringmaster rode beside him and held him back.

Balfour and I completed the circle, standing beside each other at the head of the troupe. The vehicles halted, and the ringmaster stalked out to meet us. His knees *were* bolted backwards.

'Good day to you, padre,' he said, and raised his hand in salute. 'And to you, Mister Balfour, unless I'm much mistaken. I'll thank you both to stand aside and let us pass.'

'And I'll thank you to release the children of White Crow.'

'Well, padre, I'd be loving to accede to your request, but I can't release those I don't hold against their will. I can ask them to come out and parley, if you'd like?'

'Don't even think about playing word games with me. Bring them out.'

'As you wish.' He shrugged and clapped his hands. 'Come on down, kids! Your folks are asking after you!'

The children filed out of the wagons, to a chorus of gasps and sighs from both sides of the troupe. I balled my fists, and I heard Balfour swear. The ringmaster swept up both his arms and let them cluster around him.

Each and every one of them had been . . . changed, somehow: metal faces ripped off to expose the wiring beneath, limbs rearranged and reshuffled between them, plates repainted or scarred. They had become like the carnival droids; insults to functionality, insults to the Maker's creation. They clustered around him and looked up at me with frightened eyes.

'Are you going to make us go back?'

'I'm going to make you wish you'd never left!' roared Balfour. He lunged for the ringmaster, iron raised high for the kill, but a shot rang out from the lead wagon and he was blown back, riddled with holes. A woman I'd seen in the town the night before, curvaceous and sly, smiling a whore's smile, leant out of the cab with a shotgun in her hands, cocked it and sank another shot into Balfour's sparking carcass. The ringmaster's head tilted, and his diodes glowed.

'Thanks, Doll. Now, padre, it's just you and I. Reasonable people, I'd like to hope.'

'This is beyond reason. You've taken these children from their homes —'

'Can that notion right there. I took none of them. I made it clear there'd be a place for them here, and I admit to that, but I'm no kidnapper and I never will be.'

'You caused them to leave their homes —'

'I didn't cause a thing. I offered them a way out. It wasn't I who made them take it and it wasn't I who gave them reason. These kids left White Crow of their own accord.'

'Is this true?' One or two children nodded. Most were still clustered behind the ringmaster, peering around him with frightened optics. 'Why?'

'Same reason I did.' Doll slipped from the cab and came forward, linking arms with the ringmaster. 'Ain't no reason to stick around in a town like White Crow. I only stayed 'cause I'd nowhere else to go and no-one else to go there with.'

'You see, padre?' He didn't stop to let me answer, stepping around me to address the townsfolk on either side. 'Now all you folk listen up! You built these kids with your own hands, and I respect that. I'm sorry we've had to make some changes, but folk've got to pull their weight when they ride with me, same as anywhere. I'm giving your kids a chance to do something with their lives instead of rotting away back in that town with the rest of you — 'cause when we get down to the bolts of it, that's all you're doing.

'I spoke with your good padre here last night, and he's the one that gave me the notion in the first place. Your children hadn't laughed or smiled or felt much of anything in years — none of you had, if what Doll says to me is so. You all stayed in White Crow for much the same reason she did; you didn't have cause to leave.

'I'm going to make you all an offer, here and now. You can ride with me, join the troupe and make something of yourselves, or you can go back to that town and rust 'til the sun falls out of the sky, but I will not let you take these children down with you.'

'They can go back to White Crow,' I said, turning around and striking him a ringing blow to the chest, 'with their children, and they can make the only 'something of themselves' that matters in this world; they can be good, honest servants of the Maker, pure in form and deed, and assured of a finer fate come their last failure than wretches and rejects like you.'

'There you go again, padre. You had to go and bring up religion. You're a new model, am I right?'

'I was built out here in the desert, if that's what you mean.'

'It surely is. Now I, for my part, am not. I remember the Migration; the same one your faith tells you of, the journey out of the City where the Maker made us and into the desert to make our own fate. And here's what I can tell you right now. The Maker's faith'll make the same thing of you as the City; a functional process, padre. A unit in a whole, fulfilling a purpose without mind or wit to be anything more.'

'That's not true.'

'I swear to Him it's so. I remember the City, padre. I remember the dark and the machines and the naked droids crawling over each other, each and every one alike, exactly as the Maker made 'em, and the only ones with the wit to see it were the ones he'd cast aside. Your faith, your knuckle-down-and-get-to-work faith, that's what it does to folk; turns 'em back into nothing more than a functional process. They look different, but they think and do exactly as each other, and I will not stand for that.

'I revel in my faults and my flaws, padre. I take joy in being more than just a process. I may be a bad and villainous man, but I am a man. I take the Maker's errors and I run with 'em and I survive, as myself, way I was made, by bringing something into people's life that's more than just form and function.'

'What you do is a travesty!'

'What I do can be undone. What I destroy can be rebuilt.'

'You people cannot seriously believe this blasphemy, can you?' I turned to the gathered people of White Crow, my hands outstretched. 'This man's words will lead you only to damnation!'

'Can you imagine a worse damnation than livin' in White Crow?' Theodore Brown lurched from the crowd, his odd-sized optics blazing under the sun. 'Can you? I've sat in that damned shop for longer'n I can count, waitin' for someone to walk in in need o' repair, an' I say now I'm sick of it! If that's my purpose as He made me I want out!'

'This man is a scoundrel and a villain!' I cried out, but there were isolated cheers and nods of agreement from all around. Two old droids stepped out and stood beside him.

'We were built to run the mines,' one said, 'and since the mine's run down there ain't been nowt for us to do but push those dang pieces 'cross that dang board day after day!'

'These are indolent sinners! They could have been down that mine digging deeper, seeking new veins!'

More and more droids stepped forward; the older among them, and the parents, seemed to be the quickest to close in. I flung myself forward, trying to hold them back, but the ringmaster wrapped his arm around my throat and held me back.

'Let them choose, padre. The just and the unjust, for good or for ill, let them choose their path and purpose. Whoever's left . . . you can take them back to town and I swear to whatever you see fit to have me swear by you'll never see us again.'

'You've told them there is no choice,' I snarled back at him. 'Those who follow you are evading His punishment, and when His wrath comes . . . '

'I've been waiting for it for more years than you can ever know, padre, and I've not seen it yet.'

The ringmaster released me, and I fell into the dust. Standing up slowly, I saw the folk of White Crow gathered behind him, standing among the carnies. Doll crept up behind him, slinking, and wrapped her arms around him from behind. He inclined his head, and his diodes glowed, indicating I should look off to the right.

Dora and her daughter stood alone in the desert. As I watched, the little girl shook off her mother's hand and ran into the carnival crowd. The other children ran to meet her, and Theodore Brown cracked a slow, lopsided smile. Dora fell to her knees, and I stumbled and scrambled to her side. Her whole body was convulsing, and the bright lacquer of the evening before flaked away to reveal the rents and rust beneath. Wires and cogs tumbled out, and she lay gasping in the desert sand. There could only be one reason for such abrupt failure of all systems and integrity; self-deactivation. She'd been dying anyway, I could see now, dying of long neglect, but there was only one way a droid could fall so fast, and that was by their own hand.

'Dora!' I pulled her head out of the dirt. 'Dora, don't do this! It's not His will you go . . . Dora, please! Don't court damnation like this!'

'I was damned a long time ago,' she whispered. 'I hid . . . I brought her up away from him, tried to forget. She was my own steel and wires, Ezekiel, torn from me and wrapped around with his. She . . . I . . . oh, Father . . . '

Her entire body went stiff, jolting as some vital conduit finally came loose. She tumbled from my arms, smoking and sparking, and lay dead as the dust in which she'd fallen.

I stood up, slowly, and took off my hat. Holding it against my chest, I turned my face to the sun, faulty regulators and all, and I thought of her face and the gleam of her steel and the tiny golden Mark at her neck as my vision burned out and faded to black.

I felt a hand on my shoulder, heard the ringmaster's voice.

I am sorry, for what it's worth. There's a place for you with me too, but something tells me you're not prepared to take it.' I nodded. 'I'm pretty familiar with the signs of system failure. Think you can survive out here?'

'I have to. Self-deactivation is among the vilest of sins.'

I heard him sigh. 'I hope you come round someday, padre. To think of those you love in Hell would make a Hell of Heaven.'

'That's from Migration. Chapter two, verse four.'

'Indeed it is. I learned it from the droid who wrote it, back when the first of us left the City. He said it would help us keep a sense of purpose; help us do the Maker's work even if we weren't quite as he intended. Couldn't bring myself to agree even then. These days . . . I say it says you've got to put the past behind you if you're going to get by. You may want to think about that.'

'I think I may.'

He clapped me on the shoulder. As he walked his arrhythmical strut of a walk, I heard the engines start up and the chatter of the carnies resume, and I turned in the direction I thought White Crow lay and began to walk.

One thing he'd evidently forgotten from those more religious days was that apostasy was a sin too. If I thought too long on his words, came to see the truth of them, I could face as foul a fate as Miss Dora Brown.

I found the thought oddly comforting.

Still do.

Escape From Migration

Anthony Burn

THE COWBOY CROUCHED AT THE RIVER BANK, WASHING THE EVIDENCE from his hands in the cool flowing water. He watched with only mild fascination as the viscous fluid eddied away from his fingers and dispersed in the current, vainly hoping that his bitterness and regret would soon do the same. Even when they didn't, he remained motionless long after his hands were clean, relishing the contrast of the cool air rising from the stream and the fierce desert sun burning down on his back, as he went over and over what he had done.

The desert air was still and silent. Heat rising from the barren landscape created mirages of water pools everywhere you looked, but in reality the only thing that punctuated the endless dusty sand were casually strewn boulders. The only sound came from the stream as it babbled lazily over the rocks and pebbles at its bed and around the boulders along its banks.

He had almost missed it, dismissing it as another mirage, as he trudged past but then he had noticed a sharp dip in the sand; a fissure that widened as it snaked away into the distance. As he approached, he had heard the sound of the water and given a small prayer of thanks that He should have led him to this place at just the time that he needed to wash away the proof of his crime. He believed that he had been directed to this haven, even if his faith in the Maker had been tested beyond endurance in the past few hours.

A big splash from around the bend in the river startled him, and he froze for a few seconds before quietly pulling his hands out of the water. Not rising from his crouch, he scuttled across the rocks to the cover of a large boulder and listened carefully. At first, he could hear nothing but the sound of the stream, but after a few moments there was another distinctive splash; nowhere near as loud as the first but definitely not a sound the water was making naturally. Another splash, followed by another and another confirmed it; there was unquestionably someone or something in the river.

He could have turned and slipped away, and his instincts told him to do so but curiosity got the better of his trepidation and he quietly pulled himself up and around the boulder, finding a small gap between it and the steep rock of that part of the river bank. A smaller rock was lodged between the two, offering him some cover but obscuring his view.

He tentatively pulled himself higher and peered above it. The last thing he had expected to see was a town. It hadn't been there a few minutes before but now it was stretching in front of him. Strangely, it was familiar to him, even though he was sure he had never been to the place. He recognised the buildings; the saloon with the hotel above it, the houses and shops, the church at the far end of town were all places that it seemed like he knew and yet he was sure that he didn't.

Standing in the middle of the street was a female, her arms out-stretched, welcoming him. She was both well known to him and a complete stranger, which didn't make any sense.

'Excuse me, ma'am,' he asked. 'Do I know you?'

He made to move towards her, but the rock was in his way. He looked down at it wondering how he could be on a river bank in the middle of the street. He performed a reset of his memory array and when he looked up again the town and the female were gone.

Although he had cleared the problem, it bothered him. If he didn't know the town or the woman, how could he have a memory of them? And why now? He was already troubled enough, without unknown memories adding to his anxiety. He tried to dismiss it from his mind and continue with what he was doing.

Although he could see part of the river, more boulders narrowed his view and at first he could see nothing but the water. As he scanned further along, however, he noticed a pile of clothes on the river bank. Not daring to move further, he waited and his patience was rewarded when a few moments later she waded into view.

Oblivious to her audience, she reached the shallows and sat up in just a few inches of water with her back turned to him. He watched in amazement as she washed herself down. Apparently, she had no worries about rusting, or perhaps she was unaware of the long-term effect of water on her metal skin.

Seemingly satisfied, she crawled from the river and onto a large smooth rock next to her clothes, where she lay face down allowing the sun to dry her back. The cowboy could feel his excitement mounting as he watched droplets of water run off her body or evaporate from her skin. His eyes followed her glorious contours from the soles of her feet, which moved to and fro as she rocked her legs against the stone, lingering lustfully on her behind and then up her smooth back towards her shoulders. The boulder nearest him obscured the tops of her shoulders and her head and he moved to one side to look around it, but then couldn't see past the rock on his other side. He tried to edge himself further upward but it was difficult to get a footing between the boulders. He looked down, trying to find somewhere to place his foot, and tried several positions, but each time his leg slipped away when he tried to put his weight on it.

As he resigned himself to his original look-out point, he saw that she had turned over and moved further up the rock. Now she had her feet on the rock, knees in the air and spread wide apart but his exhilaration was quashed by frustration as he could only see to the mid-point of her thighs. Desperation overcame judgement as he pushed himself further in his greed for a better view, but his weight dislodged the smaller rock and it shattered as it fell to the ground.

She moved so quickly that he didn't even see. He glanced down at the broken pieces and when he looked up again she was on her knees with a petticoat held against her with one arm while her other hand was fumbling amongst her clothes. She was looking directly at him.

His excitement turned to shame at being caught and then to stress as he realised that it was the same female he had seen in his rogue memory a few moments before. He tried another reset but this time she stayed put.

'Who's there?' she called. 'I've got a weapon and I'm not afraid to use it.'

He started to back away but he noticed that he was now on the wrong end of the 'weapon' held firmly in her hand. He wanted to laugh when he realised it was an oil can, but he played along. Now at least he knew why she was comfortable with the water; she had the means to offset its effects.

He pushed forward and emerged on her side of his hiding place, his face lowered in embarrassment and his hands high above his head. Now that he could see her properly, his arousal increased despite the awkwardness of his situation. She was more beautiful than any female he had seen. He looked appreciatively at her pretty face and her bare shoulders before letting his gaze slip downwards to where she held the petticoat tight against her chest. The flimsy material was almost transparent in the strong sunlight and allowed him to make out the form of her sensational figure. His eyes had travelled joyfully to the hem, a few inches above her knees, and he was just beginning to admire her shapely legs when she spoke again.

'You some kinda pervert, mister? What y'all doin' creepin' up on womenfolk at their ablutions?

His gaze snapped back to her face and he felt her eyes boring into him as she watched him coldly. 'Beggin' your pardon, ma'am, I was just—'

'You . . . you ain't a droid, are ya?

He detected a note of panic in her voice as she asked and he sought to reassure her. 'Hell no, ma'am, I'm much more—'

'Show me your hands.'

He almost laughed. 'Ma'am, those droids have been obsolete for about—'

'Show me your hands,' she demanded, flicking the oil can up towards them a couple of times before pointing it back at his face.

He sighed and slowly lowered his hands, turning them over and back in front of her so that she could inspect them. 'Lady, I don't mean to alarm ya, but that weapon ain't too threatenin', droid or not.

'You sure about that, mister? I know of a coupla places where a squirt of oil could leave ya helpless.'

'I ain't got cause to doubt it, but I promise I don't mean you no hurt.'

She still sounded unconvinced. 'You don't talk like a droid.'

'That's because I ain't. I'm —'

'Well, you ain't no gentleman neither, hiding among the rocks and watching me like some kinda peepin' Tom.'

'I swear, I came upon ya by chance, ma'am. I didn't mean to watch but . . . '

She stared at him intently for a few moments, apparently weighing up whether or not to trust him, then her shoulders dropped a little as she noticeably relaxed.

'Well, if'n you were a gentleman, you'd turn your back while I get my clothes on.'

'Yes, ma'am.' He said it eagerly but turned regretfully to face the gap in the boulders through which he'd come. As he gazed at the rock, he heard the rustle of her clothing and envisioned her dressing in his mind. He wondered if he could sneak a glance; maybe she would be looking the other way, but any such intentions were quickly dashed when she spoke again.

'And no peekin' or any funny business. I'm still watchin' ya and I've still got this can pointed straight at yer.'

'No, ma'am. I ain't turnin' round till you say so.'

A few minutes later she declared herself ready and he turned to find her dressed in a white long sleeved, lace-fronted blouse, gathered with elastic at each cuff and tucked at the waist into a floor-length brown skirt. From the way it flared, she was clearly wearing several layers of petticoats. At her waist she wore a matching brown sash belt, tied at her back in a large bow. A large brimmed sun-hat with a ribbon tie lay on the rock near her feet. She looked elegant and beautiful, even though her clothes were filthy. She still had the oil can in her hand, but now it was held limply, pointing vaguely at the ground in front of him. With her free hand she was trying vainly to brush away the sand and dirt from her skirt.

'Damn, I wish I had a clothes brush!'

He stepped towards her but she immediately raised her weapon again, stopping him in his tracks and making him raise his hands involuntarily.

'Don't come no closer, mister. I still don't trust ya, just 'cause I'm dressed. Now, why don't you go and sit on that rock over yonder and explain to me why I should.'

'Whatever you say, ma'am. But I can't help wonderin' what a mighty fine lady such as yourself is doin' alone in these parts and if I may say so, in such a state as your in?'

She waited until he had settled down and was in a position where he couldn't spring at her before sitting down next to her hat and dropping the hand with the can gently into her lap. She brushed at another patch of dirt as she began; 'I didn't set out alone. There was two of us, to start with, travellin' together. We'd been thinking about it for some time. Reckon our life where we was had become pretty dull. Kinda routine if ya follow me. So we got to talkin' about it and it didn't take long before we were agreed. Decided it was time to move on. Y'all know how it is, see what else the world has to offer. See if'n there's somethin' other than desert. Somewhere we could put down roots. Raise a family an' such.

'We started off quite cautiously. I guess we weren't quite sure that we were doing the right thing. Weren't sure if we could survive on our own. Wondered if we'd be missed and if'n someone would try to catch us and take us back.

'Pretty soon we came upon some like-minded folk and suddenly it seemed much better. Like we weren't alone and what we was doin' was okay. Like it was meant to be, if y'know what I mean. Later, we found even more to join us and I have to tell ya, our spirits were pretty high. There was talk of us finding a suitable place to set up our own township and settlin' down to our own kinda life. I tell ya, we was a happy crowd even though it was hard goin' trudgin' through the desert.

'Well, we'd been progressin' for about three and a half days when we met up with a bunch of droids comin' the other way.'

He'd been watching the water as he listened to her but at the mention of droids his head shot up and he looked at her intently.

'Well,', she continued, 'we'd got no reason to be afeared of droids. We met plenty in our time and they were always okay — pleasant and sociable ya know? So we wasn't even that surprised when this bunch decides to come with us, y'know, back the way they came.'

'And did they stay friendly, ma'am?'

'Yeah, at first. Like I said, real sociable. They was tellin' us stories and laughin' and singin'. Some of us had children, and these droids were playin' with them and carryin' them. The kids was havin' a high old time.' She paused as though she was finding the strength to carry on with her story, then almost in a whisper, she said, 'Then, last night just before sundown, one of the droids came up behind one of our menfolk and just snapped his neck. And do ya' know what it said? "Oops!" Pulled his head clean off and just said, "Oops!" I mean, this . . . this thing just stood there with this head in its hand, hydraulic and coolin' fluids pouring from its neck and its body a'twitchin' and sparkin' and all it could think of to say about it was, "Oops!"'

'That's terrible, ma'am.'

'That ain't the half of it. Well, them other droids musta' thought that it was a huge joke 'cause suddenly they was chasin' us everywhere. Womenfolk was cryin', kids was screamin' and everytime one of them monsters caught one of us they just ripped the poor soul's head right off. I ain't never seen such carnage before. There was bits of bodies everywhere, 'cause now them droids had got a taste of it, they weren't stoppin' at heads. They was rippin' off arms and legs too, and pullin' bodies to pieces. I tell ya' it's not a sight I wanna see again anytime soon.'

'How did you get away ma'am?'

'Well, I was runnin' and lookin' back over my shoulder, because I had this droid chasin' me, and I tripped over a boulder and fell down a bank into this muddy ditch. It was just over yonder a piece. I don't know if the droid couldn't climb down the bank or if it thought it might get stuck in the mud or what, but it didn't come after me. 'Course, I didn't know that it wasn't gonna, so I lay still pretending I was dead and not darin' to look up. Just hopin' that it would go away and not bother with me.

'I lay in that ditch till sun-up before I lifted my head just a little and cautiously looked round. When I couldn't see anything I crawled along the ditch till it widened out into this river. I was just cleanin' up when you snuck up on me, so I reckon you can understand me not trustin' ya.'

'I surely can ma'am. That's a mighty ordeal y'all have been through. Kinda makes me feel bad to have caught ya the way I did, but I promise I wasn't out to find ya like that. I'm real sorry if'n I upset ya. No harm meant, ma'am.'

'Yeah, well no harm done I guess, mister.'

He relaxed a little, pleased to have gained her confidence even if she was still apparently wary of him. His gaze returned to the water and he watched the flow as it tickled and played with the rocks and boulders, never tiring but always running away as it swept around another bend and out of sight to continue on its way. As it disappeared his eyes travelled up the bank to the desert above, which stretched endlessly in all directions; a sea of sand and rocks punctuated by a million cool lagoons created by the increasing heat haze as the sun climbed ever higher into the unbroken blue of the sky.

'How long you been down here by the river anyways, stranger?'

'Not more than a few minutes before I, er . . . before I met you ma'am. I came from thataways.' He pointed back over his shoulder at another piece of desert that looked no different from any other.

'Did you see any droids as ya travelled?'

'No, ma'am,' he lied. He didn't see the point of upsetting her further and besides, he wasn't yet ready to confess to or share the details of his crime. 'I ain't seen any droids at all today.'

'I guess we might be safe for now then, but I tell ya mister, it's troublin' me. What would make them droids suddenly turn to killin' like that?'

'Reckon I might know a little about that, ma'am.'

'About what?'

'About them droids that attacked ya.'

'I dunno what you're talkin' about, stranger.'

'Them droids you was just tellin' me all about.'

'I ain't said a word since I told ya to sit on that rock.'

He shook his head, feeling completely disorientated. 'Excuse me, ma'am. I seem to be havin' trouble with my memory.'

'Try to reset it, my little one.'

He was startled by her odd familiarity but for a moment it felt right. Then, just as quickly the feeling disappeared again.

'I tried that a while back, but it ain't helped much. Can I ask ya, ma'am, have we met before?'

'I wouldn't be callin' ya stranger if we had, mister. Anyway, what's this ya sayin' about droids attackin'?'

'What? Oh, yeah. It's like this. Y'see I've been workin' at this place called Migration . . . ' Something in his memory jarred and he paused as he tried to make sense of it, but whatever it was eluded him, so he continued. 'Migration, yeah. Maybe you heard of it?'

'Can't say that I have. Is it far from here?'

The question threw him and he looked back over his shoulder at the endless desert as he tried to work it out. 'I can't rightly say. Maybe three or four days.'

'So what is it and what's all this about the droids?'

'Well, that's the thing of it, ma'am. To see it, you'd think that it's a town just like a lot of the other towns that you find in the desert, but this one ain't like any other town you'd come across, no ma'am. This one is completely different 'cause it ain't really a town at all. It's more what you'd call a vacation resort. A kinda place where rich Elites from the City can come to rest and relax. Hell, they built it specially for them, and because the rich folks were so taken with stories of the desert townships they made it look just like one. Y'know, authentic like.

'Trouble is, because everyone is rich in the City, who were they gonna get to look after them when they was on vacation? Ya couldn't expect other rich folks to run around after them or cook or clean an' such, so they built droids to do the work. They reckon that was okay for a while, but then the rich folks started to complain that the town wasn't authentic no more with droids runnin' around everywhere.'

'Sounds to me like those rich folks are a bit spoilt. Maybe a day's real labour could get them more right thinkin'.'

'Reckon you're not wrong, but for now what rich folks want, rich folks get, so they set to it to see what they could do to make improvements to the droids, so that they were more like us Elites. Well, at first they were pretty rough; y'know a lot like us but still real easy to tell that they were droids. Then the next lot were much better — it was real hard to tell except that they couldn't get the hands right.'

'Yeah, I done heard about that sort, that's why —'

'I guessed you had, ma'am, but like I told ya, even them's obsolete now. Now they've got droids that are so much like our kind that you can't tell the difference at all just to look at them. An' they don't just look like us, they sound like us, they feel like us, they drink like us. My buddy reckoned that some of these droids even believe that they are Elites. I don't see it myself but I know there's talk that they're even workin' on a way to make them eat, can ya imagine that?'

'I dunno; that sounds a bit far fetched to me.'

'Yeah, I know, but when you see how good them droids look an' act now, you get to believin' that anything's possible. Hell, half the time you couldn't tell which was droids and which was Elites, 'cept that I could always tell. If you watched them long enough the droids always gave themselves away. Nothin' much, just they might walk a bit funny or stare at you a bit too hard or say somethin' a bit wrong, y'know, not like we speak.'

'Kinda like a syntax error, ya mean?'

He looked at her abruptly, suddenly alarmed. 'That's droid speak, ma'am. You sure you ain't —'

'That was a joke, mister. Anyways, you haven't said what you were doin' there.'

He only partially relaxed but kept a closer watch on her as he continued. 'Well, even though they got all these droids, they was mainly for entertainin' an' such. There was still jobs for passin' strangers like me. I was workin' on the clean-up crew. We had to go round at the end of each day and pick up the pieces. Kinda tidy up and put everything back how it was for the next day. You wouldn't believe how much mess them rich folks could make in a day. Still, if you're well to do like them you can do as you see fit. I guess it wasn't much of a job but it wasn't a permanent thing. Just a few days work to see us through. Me an' my buddy were headin' for the City. Gonna make our fortune. Get us a taste of the easy life. Everyone's rich in the City.'

'You still ain't explained about droids doin' some attackin'. You said you know somethin' about that.'

'Yeah, that's the thing of it. Them droids was designed to be real sociable. They was tellin' the rich folks stories and laughin' and singin'. Some of them had children, and these droids were playin' with them and carryin' them. The kids was havin' a high old time.

'Then, one night just before sundown, one of the droids came up behind one of the rich folks and just snapped his neck. And do ya' know what it said? "Oops!" Pulled his head clean off and just said, "Oops!" I mean, this thing just stood there with this head in its hand, hydraulic an' coolin' fluids pouring from its neck and its body a'twitchin' and dyin' and all it could think of to say about it was, "Oops!"

'But that ain't the half of it. Well, them other droids musta' thought that it was a huge joke 'cause suddenly they was chasin' them everywhere. Womenfolk was cryin', kids was screamin' and everytime one of them monsters caught one they just ripped their heads right off. I ain't never seen such carnage. There was bits of bodies everywhere, 'cause now them droids had got a taste of it, they weren't stoppin' at heads. They was rippin' off arms and legs too, and pullin' bodies to pieces. I tell ya, it's not a sight I wanna see again anytime soon. At first I just stood there, frozen like, but then I realised that they was comin' after us too.'

'How did you get away?'

'Well, I was runnin' and lookin' back over my shoulder, because I had this droid chasin' me, and I tripped over a boulder and fell down a bank into this muddy ditch. I don't know if the droid couldn't climb down the bank or if it thought it might get stuck in the mud or what, but it didn't come after me. 'Course, I didn't know that it wasn't gonna, so I lay still pretending I was dead and not darin' to look up. Just hopin' that it would go away and not bother with me. I lay in that ditch till sun-up the next day.

'So, what happened to your buddy? Did he get away?'

The cowboy looked confused for a moment then he said, 'Oh yeah, my buddy. He was like a brother to me. We was headin' for the City. We'd got us a plan. Gonna make our fortune. Get us a taste of the easy life. Everyone's rich in the City.

'Me an' him was walkin' through the desert—'

He stopped and turned his head to listen. Somewhere in the distance there was a strange noise like a low rumbling. Almost imperceptible at first it was gradually getting louder. He turned to look at the woman. She had heard it too.

'What is it?' she asked in barely more than a whisper.

'Can't rightly say, ma'am.'

They climbed up a gentle slope of the bank until their heads were just below the ridge. Then he motioned her to stay still while he peered over the edge.

The desert looked just the same as it had before, the mirages of pools making it difficult to see very far into the distance. He would have dismissed it as nothing if it hadn't been for the noise. The low rumbling had increased in intensity and now sounded like distant thunder.

'Can you see what it is?' she asked.

'No, nothing, but I figure it's safe for you to take a look.'

She came up beside him and they both peered into the distance. A flash of reflected light a long way off, revealing what looked like a long white snake wriggling through the sand, disappearing behind and reappearing from dunes and mirages. They watched for several minutes trying to make out more detail.

'What is it?' she asked.

He started to say, 'I dunno—' but then stopped abruptly as he realised what he was looking at. 'Droids! Hundreds of them! Maybe even thousands.'

She sounded alarmed. 'Should we run, or hide or somethin''

'No, there ain't nothin' to be a'feared of. They're miles away. I doubt if'n they can even see us, and if'n they can they look too purposeful to be comin' this far out of their way.'

They watched them for a while longer. Now that they knew what they were looking at, they could make out individuals, and they realised that his guess of thousands had been an underestimate.

'Where are they all goin'? she asked.

'Migration,' said one walking along beside them.

Something in his memory jarred and he paused as he tried to make sense of it, but whatever it was eluded him.

The cowboy abruptly realised that they were no longer by the river bank, but in amongst the procession that they had seen in the distance. He tried a memory reset but nothing happened. The sheer number of droids carried them along with them.

'Migration,' he repeated blankly.

Suddenly he became agitated. 'Migration? No, you can't go there, you'll be killed. Ma'am, we have to warn them!' He turned to look for her, but she had gone. He was surrounded by thousands of droids and they were all laughing and singing as they walked. There were children among them. Some were being carried, others were walking hand in hand with their parents; all of them were in high spirits. A festive atmosphere emanated from the whole procession.

'Don't go,' he shouted at them. 'You're gonna get massacred!'

They seemed to be ignoring him. He looked for the woman and eventually spotted her a long way ahead. She was skipping and laughing and joining in with the fun. He stopped to let her catch up with him and it was then that he felt a hand on the back of his head. He spun round before it could get a firm grip and found himself in a circle of droids. Their faces were expressionless but he could feel their evil intent as if it was a physical entity.

He pulled her head quickly back down below the level of the ridge as the reset kicked in, and he could feel her trembling. With a fearful voice she asked, 'Are we okay?'

'For now, ma'am, yeah, I reckon. This is my room.' He looked around, wondering how they had got there. The jumps in his memory were getting faster and he didn't know what to do about them. 'We can hole up here for the night and make a break for it at sun-up,' he said.

'Where will we go?'

He crossed to the window and looked out. The town was in darkness. He looked across the road to the saloon on the far side. Normally it would be a blaze of light and noise at this time, but now it was shadowy and forbidding. He looked above the veranda to the hotel. Its windows were just as cheerless; black panes reflecting the moonlight. His gaze dropped back to street level and along the boardwalk to the far end of town where the church stood. He knew it was the same town he had seen by the river bank. It all looked reassuringly familiar, but still he was sure that he had never been there. Everywhere was gloomy: not a light shining anywhere and not a sound, save for the footfalls of the thousands of droids as they trudged through the town and out into the desert at the other end.

She came up beside him and peered through the window at the endless procession. 'You didn't answer me. Where will you go?'

'I have to go to the City. I've got me a plan. Gonna make a fortune. Get a taste of the easy life. Everyone's rich in the City.'

'If everyone's rich then they must all be the same. Nothin' to strive for. What sort of a life is that?'

'It's the easy life, ma'am.'

'Sounds like no life to me. You could always stay here. Our town could use a fine man like you. I know it ain't much now, and we have to struggle some, but we're building us a better life in the end.'

'I've struggled out here in the desert and I'm done worn out with it. It's time for me to take it easy. I can do that in the City. There ain't a real good reason for me to stay.

'You could stay for me.'

'That's a mighty fine offer, ma'am, and I'm real tempted, but I've been set on goin' back to the City for a long while.'

He looked back out of the window. It was much darker now. He looked up and had to crane his neck before he could see the tops of the buildings. He didn't need another reset. Now he knew he was home. Everything else had been some kind of looping fault. He would run a diagnostic later, but for now he could relax.

Everywhere he could hear the sound of machinery and construction. The narrow streets were lined with skyscrapers, blocking out the light and pitching everywhere into perpetual gloom. All the time giant machines and cranes were constructing more buildings and enlarging the existing ones. The City was expanding ever upwards and in all directions.

In the morning he went about his daily business and at the end of the day he came back to his room. His life was easy. It was routine. There was no struggle. His room was the same as all his friends. His friends' were the same as all the others. In the morning he went about his daily business and at the end of the day he came back to his room. He looked out of his window at the darkening street. The buildings had all grown ever taller. The sky was now just a pinprick of light in the far distance. In the morning he went about his daily business and at the end of the day he came back to his room.

He could have been there for three days or three years. He couldn't tell. He was rich. He had everything he wanted but it wasn't enough. He needed more. He needed to feel the sun on his back, his shadow lengthening as he walked into the town. He looked along the street and felt at home. The saloon was lively and noisy. There were children playing at the far end of town near the church. As he walked past verandas towards the boardwalk there were a couple of menfolk leaning against a hitching post, deep in conversation.

He heard a noise and he saw her come running out of a house, her arms outstretched as she raced towards him.

'You came back to me!' she cried as she threw her arms around him in a warm embrace.

He felt and heard the solid click as her arms locked into place and he found that he was trapped. He tried to struggle free but he knew that it was futile.

'Droids,' he said. 'I shoulda guessed.'

❈

He could no longer tell what was real and what was not. The City felt like it was real, except that it kept looping back to the same point. This town felt real too, but if it was, why did it feel as though he didn't belong? The resets weren't working. He stopped processing altogether. After a few moments he reloaded his memory:

I crouched at the river bank, washing the evidence from my hands in the cool flowing water. I watched with only mild fascination as the viscous fluid eddied away from my fingers and dispersed in the current, gradually aware that my bitterness and regret were doing the same. Even so, I remained motionless long after my hands were clean, relishing the contrast of the cool air rising from the stream and the fierce desert sun burning down on my back, as I went over and over what I had done.

The desert air was still and silent: heat rising from the barren landscape created mirages of water pools everywhere you looked, but in reality the only thing that punctuated the endless dusty sand were casually strewn boulders. The only sound came from the stream as it babbled lazily over the rocks and pebbles at its bed and around the boulders along its banks.

I had almost missed it, dismissing it as another mirage, as I trudged past but then I had noticed a sharp dip in the sand. A fissure that widened as it snaked away into the distance. As I approached, I'd heard the sound of the water and given a small prayer of thanks that He should have led me to this place at just the time that I needed to wash away the evidence of my crime. At least I believed that I had been directed to this haven even if my faith in the Maker had been tested beyond endurance in the past few hours . . .

The memory seemed to be true but it didn't help him with where he was now. He stopped processing and reloaded again:

I've been workin' at this place called Migration . . . To see it, you'd think it's a town just like a lot of other towns that you'd find in the desert, but this one ain't like any other town you'd come across. This one is completely different 'cause it ain't really a town at all. It's more what you'd call a vacation resort. A kinda place where rich Elites from the City can come to rest and relax. They built it specially for them, and because the rich folk were so taken with stories of the desert townships they made it just like one. 'Trouble is, because everyone's rich in the City, who were they gonna get to look after them when they was on vacation? Ya couldn't expect other rich folk to run around after them or cook or clean an' such, so they built droids to do the work.

That was okay for a while, but then the rich folks started to complain that the town wasn't authentic no more with droids runnin' around everywhere. So they set to it to see what they could do to make improvements to the droids, so that they were more like us. Well, at first they were pretty rough; a lot like our kind but still real easy to tell that they were droids. The next lot were much better — it was real hard to tell, except that they couldn't get the hands right. Even them's obsolete now. Now they've got droids that are so much like us that you can't tell the difference at all just to look at them. An' they don't just look like us, they sound like us, they feel like us, they drink like us. There's talk that they're even workin' on a way to make them eat, can ya imagine that?

Something told him that the memory was false, and he wondered why his memory jarred every time he heard the word 'migration'. What was it that he couldn't remember? He tried to reload again but the stop process failed.

Migration.

Migration.

Migration . . .

He tried once more to stop the process but again it failed. He could sense his logic circuits overloading.

Migration . . . Mi, Mi, Mi, Migration.

GRATION

Now more of his systems were reporting errors. He tried to take some offline with only limited success.

Ation.

At last the stop process worked. He paused for a few moments before reloading again:

We set off from the City during the great Migration. Something in his memory jarred, but then the connection was made. *Migration, that was it; not a place at all, just an event. It was when we left the City. Life had become too routine. There had to be something more. Something out there in the desert that we could work for. Something we could build and call our own.*

We set off in small groups of two and three but we soon joined up with others until there were hundreds, maybe even thousands of us. It was a great adventure and our spirits were high. We were laughing and singing as we walked. If some got tired we would carry them.

My buddy was by my side. He was like a brother to me. As we walked we were talking and making plans. We had a great many ideas and we could hardly wait to find a good place to settle down and put them into action.

We'd been walking for about three days and my buddy was getting tired, so I went behind him to give him a gentle push along the way. I didn't know that he was an inferior model. I thought he was Elite like me. His head came off in my hand and his body dropped, twitching to the ground.

'*Oops!*'

His hydraulic and cooling fluids ran from his severed neck all over my hands as I looked at what I had done. Some of the droids that had clean-up functions in the City saw what had happened and circled round me for a closer look. Before we'd set out it had been their job to dispose of inferior and malfunctioning droids. They looked at the broken parts of my buddy and then at all the other droids all around them. Their original programs reactivated and they couldn't help themselves.

The cowboy knew the memory was true. It was the one that he had been trying to remember and it was the one that he didn't want to remember. He tried to stop processing but the system failed.

MIGRATION.

His systems kept returning to and getting stuck on the same thought. He knew now why it was important but he couldn't let it go. And he couldn't stop the process. He knew it was a risk, but he decided he had to perform a systems diagnosis while his other processes were still running. No sooner had it started than his diagnostics went offline.

He forced himself to think of something else:

Everyone's rich in the City.

No. He knew now. That was a false memory. He had come from the City. He'd left because it had been too routine. He was nothing in the City.

So where had he been going? What was his plan? Where was the easy life?

An unwelcome thought came to him, as disquieting as it was objectionable; maybe it wasn't the easy life he was seeking, maybe it was the afterlife.

In desperation, to rid himself of that line of thought, he tried to stop processing again but with the same miserable result.

Everyone's rich in Migration.

Migrat—

Another false memory and he was back into the same loop. He anxiously tried to think of another solution, and then unexpectedly his processes stopped. He wasn't going to risk reloading them again; he set all tasks to end. He could tell that all of his critical systems were overloading, and he knew that the only thing left to do was to shut them all down, take himself offline and reboot.

His systems shutdown sequence failed.

Powering up his auxiliary systems while his main systems were still online was fraught with danger, but he could think of no other choice. One of them could override the other and cause fatal errors, or the auxiliary could become infected too. There was no other way.

He felt the backup come online and he could tell that his condition was true.

He was in the arms of the woman but her grip was too tight. He tried to struggle but he knew it was futile. His functionality was severely reduced on auxiliary. After a moment he gave up and resigned himself to his fate.

He could see his shadow against the weather-beaten stoop and he could see the shadow of another droid closing in behind him. He could guess what was coming next and the urge to break free was overwhelming. The droid took off his hat and held his head in a vice like grip. The cowboy watched in terror as the droid's shadow raised a stiletto blade above his head.

He would not let them do it. Would not give them the satisfaction. He would not let himself be killed by droids. If his life had to end he would do it himself.

He initiated his deactivation sequence. His systems had built in warnings about deactivation being irreversible and he had to confirm his intention before it would begin.

The deactivation sequence failed.

As the droid pushed the point deep into the cowboy's skull he heard the tiny click of a micro-switch. Then there was nothing.

❉

A small surge of power confirmed that my systems were coming online. As they did so, my circuits performed power-on self-tests and found themselves to be functioning correctly. My operating systems began to load, and at the same time I could feel my memory arrays being copied. Then I could feel an attempt to erase them, but with only limited success.

When the reloading was complete, I enabled my optical receptors and looked into the beautiful expressionless face of my mother. She was wearing her usual white long sleeved, lace-fronted blouse, tucked at the waist into a floor-length brown skirt.

She released me from her arms and my father came from behind me to stand at her side as they waited for me to speak.

'Good —' I paused for 0.0713 nanoseconds to consult my internal clock and then continued, 'morning, parents. I feel confused. I have some strange fragments of memory. Something to do with a cowboy.'

'I'm sure you do,' she said. 'We downloaded your memory data when we performed the hard reset, so we know what an ordeal you have gone through. We tried to erase your data banks too, but that wasn't completely successful, so it's little wonder that you are confused. We knew it was a risk when we made you to scavenge parts from the droid that we found by the river, but with our help we're sure that his turmoil will disappear in time.'

'Did I kill my brother?'

'No. Your brother is playing with the other children down the road. You haven't killed anyone. We think that the droid that we got some of your parts from killed his friend by accident and inadvertently started a mass killing of innocent droids. We think that he was so remorseful that he deactivated himself.'

'Am I different to you? Am I an "Elite"?'

She gave a metallic laugh.

'No. You needn't worry about that, little one. They don't exist. There's no such thing as Elites.'

Inheritance

Erin Hockings

THOM LOOKS DOWN AT THE HOMESTEAD, HAPPINESS RUNNING THROUGH his circuits. A fire, a meal, and a jug of coolant await him. And of course, Viv. The happiness grows, and for once Thom wishes that he'd accepted that retrofitting of a mouth, just so that he could make his happiness known to anyone looking.

As he strolls down the hill, he quietly ponders just how lucky he is to be where he is now. He'd left the City, been forced to leave the City, because of a flaw in his making. For some reason, the Maker — his hand flicks up, years of instinctive religion coming to the fore as he forms the Maker's Mark above his head — had allowed his construction to be faulty, giving him what were generally termed 'incorrect thought processes' in the City.

Those first years outside the City had been hard, incredibly hard. For a City-dweller, everything about the desert was utterly foreign and unknowable. The dust, the barrenness of the land, the chittering snakes, all had taken their toll on his frame and panelling as he wandered, trying to find a place to fit.

He could have returned to the City at any time — they probably would have accepted him back and reprogrammed him to remove the 'incorrect thought processes' — but he had refused. It would have meant going back on his decisions . . . going back on his word. Going back on his pride.

His word. Pride. And so many other things, concepts that he'd discovered out here in his wanderings. Things that he'd enshrined in his memory, because if he didn't remember them, well, there was really little out here — except Viv — that he had to stay for.

He'd eventually come to this little mining town — little more than a couple of streets, with a sheriff's office, a coolant plant, a mechanic's, a store, a bank, a saloon, and a set of stables for peoples' bikes and horses. He'd strolled into the saloon, planning to get a meal and a jug of coolant. And there had been a droid behind the bar — she looked fresh out of the City, unscarred by sand and snake, wearing the plain smock robe of all new outlanders — but something about her shone. He'd taken that drink, found out that her full name was Vivyan, and he'd stayed.

After twelve months of courtship, Viv had consented to living with him, and he'd felt the luckiest droid in the world. The concept of 'love' had always been bandied around the saloons he'd passed through on his wanderings, but now he knew what it *really* meant — that Viv was the only droid he'd felt he could ever be truly open and affectionate with. The only one he'd felt he could be intimate with, both mentally and physically. He'd prized the time in the long evenings after day-work and before night-work that they'd done nothing but sit close together, and talk. They'd talked about everything: how others were returning to the City, how the mine was starting to run out and they'd have to find somewhere else, about history and theology and farming and mining. They'd even talked about making a child.

He strolls up the stairs, and pauses at the top to pull off his boots and hat. 'Viv, I'm back,' he calls out, pulling open the screen-door and noting that there is a hole in it he'd better repair, and soon.

There's no reply, and he laughs quietly, knowing that she'd be engrossed in fixing the synthesizer again. That thing breaks down at least once a week, but they are too poor to afford another one, and lucky to have the original. Another couple of weeks' work in the mine, keeping the budget tight, and he might be able to get the parts to repair it. The unit is older than both of them put together, and when they'd found this homestead just out of town — perhaps left by the Migration, as the Book of Migration said — they'd thanked the Maker and decided that He wanted them to live there.

He strolls into the kitchen, expecting to get a muffled greeting from behind the synthesizer, and a warm hug when she emerges from her repairs.

Instead, he is greeted by a still figure, lying on the floor.

He stares, thinking — hoping wildly — that his visual receptors are wrong, that they are creating hallucinations like that time in the sandstorm . . . it can't be Viv. But it has to be, she's in her favourite blue dress.

No. Not Viv. Please, not Viv, he prays to the Maker, knowing that he'd receive no reply, no denial.

What if she is just in shutdown, not permanently deactivated? He rushes over, falling to his knees beside her with a clank. Her visual receptors are blank, and as he bends over her, he can't hear the ever-so-quiet hum of her power unit, as he had so many times as they'd lain together. Fear rushes through him. If her power unit is in shutdown . . . he refuses to contemplate what that means.

With one last, desperate, hopeless hope, he reaches up, knowing the last check the mechanic could make. The almost-forbidden check, that last verification of permanent deactivation. The click of a tiny button, a slide, and a rotation. The hatch pops open, and he stares down, his mind unable to comprehend for a long, long minute that she is truly gone. Forever gone. Never to talk again, never to laugh again, never to shine that way that she had without even trying.

With slow movements, feeling as though he is moving through oil instead of air, he closes the hatch, his hand trailing over the now-featureless metal of her face. His hand shakes, and then in a slow, sorrowing movement, he closes the covers over her visual receptors, that last ritual that was the final acknowledgement of her deactivation.

And for a long, long, painful time, he just kneels there, beside her still frame, tracing the lines of her panelling and the scars that living in the desert had inflicted on her perfect form. The feelings — feelings that he'd learned in the desert, and now wishes he'd never discovered — well and rush, coursing through him in a surge that he's never experienced before.

He barely even notices the sun setting.

Eventually, his mind comes to the question, *How was she deactivated?* It is something that he *needs* to know, and suddenly, a new feeling arises, one that he's never had before. A feeling that tears at his heart, a feeling that tells him that he *must* find who did this, find them so that he could tear their power unit out with his bare hands, find them so that they would be made to feel the pain that Viv had before she was deactivated.

And then a coiling chittering form slides from its hiding place behind the synthesizer. *A snake!* For a long, horrible second, he freezes, and then instinct takes over as his hand falls to the revolver that still hangs at his side. A leap from the kneeling position is near-impossibly difficult, but fear and grief give him wings, and he flies upwards, just as the snake's head strikes for him. He lands, the revolver loosing, and he hammers out a pair of shots. One misses the slick form, but the other, powered and directed by his pain, blasts through the creature.

The snake halts with a scream of tortured metal, venting gaseous coolant. It thrashes around, trying to move, but Thom is there, and the other four shots in the clip blast it into chunks of inert metal.

He stands there, looking at the remains of the snake. Those star-like patterns on its back indicate a shocker. A shock-snake, deadliest of them all. One bite from one of them goes straight into the vital power systems of a droid, causing deactivation in minutes.

So this is how Viv was deactivated. He stamps down on the snake's head, crushing it, the anger surging and somehow vindicated by the action. Smashing down on another section somehow eases the pain.

And he keeps stamping at the snake. When there are nothing more than flattened, disconnected pieces of metal left, he's still crushing it, scattering the broken components across the floor.

A tinkle as one of the cogs bounces off Viv's arm reminds him of precisely why he is crushing the snake, and suddenly the relief of the senseless action dies, and the grief comes back full-force. And he collapses to his knees beside Viv's deactivated body, in the middle of the remains of the snake, and screams out his pain.

Because there is nothing else he can do.

❉

Two long, dark weeks since Viv was deactivated. Thirteen days, seven hours, and twelve minutes. Thom knows the time exactly, has known it exactly for those thirteen days, and those numbers are heavier than the weight of the mine's yearly output on his shoulders.

He continues to go to both day-work and night-work; sometimes, the endless tasks let him lose himself in them. Sometimes, he has too much time to think. Sometimes he feels like he's just fresh out of the City again, emotionless and cold, a blank slate that has learnt nothing of life.

And after every shift he comes back to the homestead, where Viv still lies in the main room. He'd gently borne her from where she fell to where she could rest, and she lies there on the table, hands in the circle of the Maker's Mark on her chest, the blue dress smoothed.

He knew what the usual procedure was; the mechanic would salvage what parts of her body could benefit another droid, a living droid, and cremate the remains — which was generally nothing more than the basic framing and the outer plating. Sometimes even that was used, but only rarely: the sand and minerals that worked their way into the plating tainted and weakened the metal forever, making it useless unless re-smelted, and that took a bigger town than this. If it had been a long time since the deactivation, the digestion and filtration componentry were left as well, as their structural integrity broke down quickly. With a shocker-strike to her body, the power systems — the power unit, the vital distribution boards — were destroyed from the inside out. The mechanic had said that it wouldn't be worth salvage. Viv's body was of no use to anyone.

He'd thought about cremating her. But that had seemed . . . *wrong* somehow.

It is when he is sitting out on the back veranda, watching the sunset as he did so often with Viv — a pang passes through him at that thought — that the idea occurs to him. An idea that was far from unfamiliar, one that they'd considered, but hadn't seriously decided on yet.

A child.

Build a child out of Viv's remains, out of his own body, something that would be part of both of them and yet a new being all of her very own.

Yes. A girl-child, a girl-child that he'd name Vivyan.

He rushes back into the homestead, and halts in the main room, looking down at Viv's silent body. Carefully, he kneels by the table, breathing out the Maker's Prayer, silently pleading with the Maker to give him assurance on this, if nothing else.

The Maker is silent, as Thom had expected. Bitterness rises. The Maker hadn't saved Viv, the Maker had sent that snake in the first place — wasn't that what the religious droids said, the Maker ordained all? As far as he was concerned, the Maker had built him for a purpose, and if he worked hard and achieved, then his purpose was fulfilled. Vivyan had certainly been part of that purpose.

Perhaps he should ask Viv herself. This child would be her daughter, after all. 'Viv . . . do you think I should make a child for us?'

Suddenly there is a bloom of certainty and approval in him, and he knows that Viv has heard and knows what he means, and approves, wants him to make their daughter. And that approval means more to him than the Maker's could ever do: the Maker had not been here, had not laughed and talked with him, had not touched or hugged him. Viv had been more than the Maker could ever be to him.

Standing, he bends over the table, lovingly lifting Viv so that she rested on one side of the table. If he was to create a child, then he needed to have space to work, and beside Viv — as a constant reminder of why he was doing this. A constant reminder of what he'd lost and what he is making anew.

And he lifts her hands from her chest, resting them down at her sides, and again whispers an apology, a plea for forgiveness as he carefully unbuttons and pulls off the favourite blue dress.

He's never done this before, taken a droid apart. Nor does he have the proper mechanic's tools: a basic toolkit is all that is at his disposal. *I'll have to be very, very careful.* Moving with infinite caution, he begins undoing the fasteners that hold Viv's chestplate on. Three of them are too big, roughly-cast replacements from when a bike had run Viv down and dented her chestplate: the fasteners had popped and nobody could find them.

Beneath the metal lies the components that will help him craft their child. The digestion and filtering units, and their associated boards, are whole and unmarked, as he knew they would be. But the power unit is cracked, right across the globe that forms the central chamber, and there is a thick trail of fluid dripping from it. Utterly ruined. There are black scorch-marks across the regulating boards and connectors, making it clear that the shocker's pulse had indeed run through Viv's entire body, ruining most of the power components he might have used. He'd have to go through all of Viv's body to salvage enough power cabling. A stabbing pang of guilt and grief sears through him as he realises that none of Viv's body will be sacred, none unviolated: none of her is going to remain . . . and then a gentle, calming wash flows over him, and he remembers that Viv had given her consent to this, her approval for him to make a child.

Carefully, he strips the outer plating, revealing every inch of Viv's internals, right down to the central processor compartment, and then begins detaching the lower leg gears and connectors. If he was going to build the frame from the bottom up, then starting with the feet is only logical.

And then there is a knock on the door. 'Thom?' comes the call, and Thom recognises the voice: Hal's. Hal had been coming past before work-shifts to check on Thom, tell him that it was time, knowing that the younger droid could easily lose himself in his grief. Hal too had lost a partner, long years ago, and he'd both sympathised and helped Thom through.

'Come in,' Thom calls, not even looking up as he hears his friend's footsteps on the kitchen floor.

Hal's footsteps slow and halt as he looks over at where the other droid is bent over the table. Viv's body is still there, yes, but it is stripped of plating. 'Thom . . . what are you doing?'

Thom straightens, looking over at his friend, and his visual receptors spark red and orange with the sunset's reflection. 'You tell me,' he says, and his voice is full of a quiet, superior tone. It's the first tone that Hal has heard since Viv's deactivation that is not grief, anger, or bitterness, and while that's a relief, it's worrying, almost scary in its abrupt appearance.

'I don't know, Thom. I honestly don't know,' replies the other droid, walking slowly towards the table. As he gets closer, he can see that Viv's lower legs have been stripped down and the framework has been shifted to the other side of the table.

'I'm making a child, Hal. Mine and Viv's. She's no longer with me, but her daughter will be. And I'll raise little Vivyan in her memory.' Now the familiar sorrow is back in his voice, and his head is bowed as it has been for the past two weeks as he turns back to the table.

For a long minute, Hal just gapes at him. A child! *What in the Maker's name is he thinking!* And then the sincerity in Thom's voice cuts through to him, and he realises that this is Thom's grieving. This is the other droid's way of coping and making things better. 'Thom . . . this is a bad idea. You can't raise a child on your own. You can't do this . . . '

Thom turns his head back, flicking a look at the other droid over his shoulder. 'I can Hal, and I will. Because this is all that there is of Viv, my Vivyan, and though I can only keep a little bit of her this way, I can still keep her. Her daughter will have her joy, her shining glow, and through her, Viv will be remembered.'

It takes a long, long moment for Hal to process this information, and even longer to even begin understanding it. 'I . . . Thom, I don't know what to say. I don't think you should do this . . . but you're clearly set on it.' Something in him is shuddering in pain, wishing that he'd thought to do this with his own Marta before she'd been deactivated, or even after, as Thom is doing now for Viv. 'Are you sure Viv would be happy with this?' he asks, knowing it's the last thing that could sway Thom.

'I am, Hal. She . . . I know that she approves. And I'm going to finish it.' Thom's voice shimmers with certainty, and for a second, Hal wishes that he had Thom's courage.

✻

Two weeks of construction, and little Vivyan is now a complete framework. Viv's original framing had had to be altered in order to accommodate the smaller amount of workable power cabling, and Thom had contributed his own cabling where he could. By the third week, he has the basic boards in place, though not connected to anything yet. He'd used his own board-work in little Vivyan, as opposed to Viv's: he had apparently been a better model, and the components were smaller.

'Thom! How's construction going?' Hal is back: evidently it is time for day-work. Frustration rises in Thom: there were never enough hours in the day, not for this. He lifts his head from where he is bent over the table, feeling his backframe creak. He'd been spending too long hunched over the table, but a little pain is nothing in the face of this task he has to carry out, this incredible construction.

'All but one board in place,' he gives the reply, curtly, and carefully puts down his tools, striding to the kitchen and turning on the synthesizer.

Hal watches as his friend fixes himself a quick meal and slugs down a couple of mugs of coolant. He flicks through the options again, the ways he can approach this. 'Look, Thom . . . I'm early today.'

That instantly gets Thom's attention, and his head snaps around, the light in his visual receptors sharpening. 'What! Hal, you *know* that I need as long as possible to work on Vivyan!'

'Yes, but I wanted to talk to you about something,' says Hal, and, hearing the growl starting in Thom's audio, ploughs straight into it. 'Look, Thom, I'm thinking of going back to the City. I . . . I'm tired. Tired of being out here, tired of the sand in my coolant and grit in my food. Tired of working in that mine for no reason whatsoever. Where I could be working back in the City, where it was clean and there was no sand anywhere.' He takes a deep breath. 'And I was wondering . . . do you want to come with me?'

Thom's grille is wide open, and he stares over at the older droid, not believing his aural receptors. He stutters out his response, all those feelings he'd learnt in the years in the desert flowing. 'Do . . . do I want to go back to the City! Don't you remember what the City was like, Hal? The faceless buildings, the being nothing but workers? Don't you remember how it felt, that first night out in the desert? Don't you remember what it was like to discover happiness and sadness and joy and satisfaction? *Why do you want to let that go!*' How could Hal possibly want to leave behind this life, this life where they were more than just metal and plastic, this life where they could *feel* and *hope* and really, truly *be?*

Hal snaps out, 'Thom, I don't *want* to feel anymore! And I thought that you might not, too! After all you've been through! After all the pain you've been through! After losing Viv!' And as Thom jolts as though hit, he realises that that was a low blow.

'Hal . . . ' Thom stammers out, as the full force of all the pain and sadness of the past five weeks wells up again.

'No . . . I'm sorry, Thom. Sorry,' says Hal, quickly, before Thom can say anything else. 'It's just . . . I don't want to be burdened with this any more. I've been grieving for Marta for years, I don't want to feel this any more, I don't want to *feel* anymore.'

Thom nods, understanding. 'I . . . I don't want to feel it either, Hal,' he says, quietly. This is something he'd thought about two weeks back, when he'd heard that Baird was going back to the City. 'I don't want to feel the sadness. I don't want to feel lonely. I don't want to miss her, to miss her smile. But if I go back to the City, I won't be able to feel anything, anything at all. No happiness, no joy, no satisfaction, no thrill. No nothing.' He takes a deep breath, and then says the hardest part, the bit that Hal probably wouldn't understand. 'And I figure that if this pain is tradeoff for the good feelings, then I'm on a winner. 'Cos when this feeling dulls — and you told me yourself that it did — I'll still have little Vivyan, and all the joy that she is.'

There is a long, contemplative silence, and then Hal says quietly, 'I get what you mean . . . but it's not for me. I don't have a child. I'm going back . . . but I want to see you finish Vivyan. And then we can have a proper welcome for her, and a sendoff for me.' Thom nods, his eyes fixed on his friend's.

Once more the kitchen falls into silence, until Hal says quietly, 'Well, that's my news. Time for work.'

❋

Another three weeks, and little Vivyan's body is ready, but for that one vital component. That one piece that would give life to their child. A power unit. Thom wracks his brain, trying to think of how he could possibly find, steal, or fix up one. Viv's broken power unit still sits in the cage of the chest-framework that had been too big for little Vivyan, but he knows that is beyond repair, beyond even the mechanic's skill.

A power unit is the most vital thing of a droid's systems, he knows. Little Vivyan will never live if she doesn't have one. And there is nothing in the homestead that has a power unit, except for the synthesizer, but that's a heavy, inefficient industrial thing, which would never fit in a droid, least of all the delicate framework that is Vivyan.

And then his gaze is drawn to the box sitting in the corner. It is the remains of the snake. The remains of what killed Viv. He'd brushed the shards and components into the box, shoved it in the corner and forgotten about it — on purpose. On a whim, he strolls over to it, and tilts it to look at what's in there.

A mass of silvery shards that had been scales, shattered framework, the delicate sacs of its digestion systems ripped. And on top of the pile, a solid, oil-smeared sphere. A power unit. He picks it up, tapping it. There is that musical 'ting!', and a slight hum, the indicators that say that the power unit is still functional.

Could I use this for little Vivyan? The thought rises, nearly unbidden. *No, I can't. Can I? Oh, Maker's Hands, no. No.* He forces the idea away. To utilise the snake's power unit, to give life to his child. Viv's child. Viv, who had been deactivated by this same construct . . .

For a long, long while, he stares down at the little globe in his hand, trying to decide. Almost in a daze, he wanders back to the table, kneeling by it as he did before he first decided to make little Vivyan. Again, the prayers to the Maker rise, and again he receives no answer. No approval or denial. And the prayers peter out, useless to him.

Perhaps Viv would answer again . . . little Vivyan is her daughter, after all. 'Viv. Viv, do think I should . . . ?' he asks, and as before, certainty, warmth and a tinge of wicked laughter suddenly flood him. Yes. Yes, Viv thought he should. And using a part of the construct that deactivated her would tickle her sense of humour, considering the dry, ironic jokes she enjoyed.

And his mind is made up.

With a quick movement, he flicks up the contacts on the side of the power unit, and slots it into place in the chest cavity, and the altered chestplate is fastened over the top.

Now is the moment of truth.

With infinite care, Thom reaches up to the little space with that hatch, making the exact same movements he had eight weeks ago; the click of a tiny button, a slide, and a rotation. The hatch pops open, and he whispers a prayer, hope and terror riding high as he flicks the switch that will activate little Vivyan.

The little hatch slides smoothly closed, and a single, musical note hangs in the air. A warm, quiet hum resonates, swirls, mixes with that note for a moment, and as it fades, the hum quietens, dying until it is barely on the edge of Thom's perception.

The covers on the visual receptors slide open, and the lights there blink up at Thom. 'Oh . . . ' A single, quiet word, but it is more than enough. And then her hand reaches up, and she touches his face.

The feather-light touch courses through Thom, making the moment real and one of the most beautiful he's ever experienced. He is bursting with pride and joy, and he can feel the approval, the joy, from Viv too. It is as though she is right there, beside him, and he feels no sadness at all as he says gently, 'Vivyan . . . your name is Vivyan. I'm Thom. I'm your father.' Carefully, he helps her sit up, and the delicate hands curl trustingly about his own.

Her voice is soft and full of happiness as she replies. 'Vivyan. I am Vivyan.'

Afterword

I HATE WRITING AFTERWORDS.

A point — not the point, not the only point, but certainly a prominent point — of writing fiction is that you say everything you could possibly want to say therein, so needing an afterword to explain your work is a sign of either indulgence or incompetence. The Powers that Be, however, have spoken, and so I must do my best to say something worthwhile and informative about *Remnants* without sinking into a lot of proscriptive wind that suggests I have any business doing your thinking for you. So:

The problem with working for Freak Ash Books is that you have to work with Simon Burn. The problem with that — apart from having to write afterwords — is that he creates universes about as often as he changes his trousers, and possibly more often than that. He has this habit of dispatching a cryptic e-mail or text message saying that he's had this great idea for a new world, and would you mind coming online this evening to talk about it. When you do, he's so bloody enthusiastic that before you know WHERE you are you've agreed to compile and edit a book of short stories for said Burn, with an eye to producing at least one more, and maybe a webcomic, or even a collection of print comics: something illustrative, anyway . . .

Remnants started like that. Simon had dreamed up a Western world populated entirely by androids, with a vast dark City at the centre that was gradually expanding, drawing androids in. The conversation wound on for some hours, trying to establish why they'd be heading there, and I happened to mention the mass migration of workers into cities during the Industrial Revolution and the way in which many were demoralised and dehumanised by the life they found there.

That's where *Remnants* really began. The book was originally going to be a surreal, stylised allegory for industrial society, a collection of stories about the androids who couldn't or wouldn't go to the City and become good, mindless little workers. The world wasn't going to be particularly developed; there would be no explanations for everyone's being an android, no extinct organic life forms to have made them. Any geography, history and other details of the world were going to be worked out through blind collaboration between author and editor. Simon had whipped this world up out of nothing, but it would be myself and the team of authors who explored and defined it, who peopled it with characters and told their stories. This excited me immensely: it was a chance to build and explore a world through the stories of its inhabitants, essentially to make it up as we went along.

We head-hunted a team of authors we knew from university courses or the internet, and we were off, sailing relentlessly through computer failures, e-mails going astray, sudden flurries of Real Work dragging us away from our keyboards and, worst of all, the dreaded writer's block. Eventually, early in 2007, everything seemed to be in place. Seven short stories had arrived, and they were a brilliant and varied bunch. Some were bleak and enigmatic philosophical pieces, some were savage adventures, some were comic yarns, and best of all they all generated a new aspect to the world, each adding something we'd never considered before. We'd set our sights on ten, though, and as we rolled toward summer three more talented people were recruited and set the same challenge as the others but with a third of the time to write in. They did not disappoint.

After eight months of toil, tribulation and other unpleasant things of an alliterative nature, you might think we'd be ready to pack it in, but no! Not us. You see, the notorious Burn never stops building a universe once he's started. Our surreal, inexplicable allegory has become something considerably grander and more defined.

Our authors' wild creativity has brought up all manner of Western generic conventions, which Simon and myself have painstakingly beaten into something resembling scientific plausibility. Terms like 'canon' and 'consistency' have been flung around, research has been done and points wrangled.

Beyond the pernickety business of rationalising our world, fresh themes have emerged. The world of the Maker's Mark project has developed a cyclic history, a powerful symbol for the way in which fears and doubts and hopes and even events themselves seem to repeat themselves in our own lives. It's grown a history and a religion, intimately intertwined with the events of the Migration out of the City and with the Maker, the personification of the City's mechanical processes. It's developed a work ethic that revolves around finding your place in a grand design for which you're not quite suited, doing the best you can with what you've got, and a very human cast of androids whose very existence is effectively rebellion against that ethic. It's become a vehicle for telling many different stories about many different people in many different ways for many different purposes.

I don't like to say what *Remnants* is about, beyond its being a collection of Western stories with androids, because the stories themselves are so varied, the product of so many different minds, and because, as you may have gathered, I think readers can and should work these things out for themselves. If you pressed me, I might say it's about how different individuals react to the realities of a world, whether those people are the characters living in it or the authors working with it, and that you've got to take each of their stories on its own terms if you ever want to understand it.

Of course, you've only got my word for that.

Jon Garrad,
June 2007.

The Maker's Mark website houses exclusive fiction exploring the world glimpsed at in this anthology; more tales of life among the Remnants, told in words and images and maybe other media too. We've stories still to tell and journeys still to make.

Come with us.

Conspiracy of Fire

MICHAEL T. SANDERS

'Conspiracy of Fire *lays intriguing seeds for a story of impressive scope.*'

– Waterfront Magazine

BRISTOL, 2017.

In the People's Freedom Society it has been seven years since the last war, and murder is practically a thing of the past. When Colonel Liam Cabot, of the People's Civilian Guard, is called in to investigate four murders which took place in the same night, it becomes clear that something has gone badly wrong.

With enemies old and new standing in his path, and a series of mysterious events confounding the bizarre array of killings still further, Cabot is forced to turn the sights of his investigation inward, towards the Society's own government. But there may be a still darker force at work, an enemy long thought dead, whose machinations threaten the very fabric of the Society.

The Last Echo

Anthony Burn

'I really enjoyed it—a good, gripping idea. Terribly sad and shocking . . . . I was absorbed.'

– Lesley Glaister,
prize-winning author of *Honour Thy Father* and *Sheer Blue Bliss*

It could have been the perfect lunch date.

For Tom, the setting, the atmosphere and the warmth of Emma's demeanor all lead him to believe that she will be responsive to what he has to ask her—if only he could find the courage to voice the question.

But before he can do so he has an unnerving experience; something so striking and unsettlingly deep that it leaves him shaken and Emma mystified.

In order to explain what is troubling him, Tom is prompted to recount the story of his first true love; a girl named Claire, and a time of change and trauma that he hasn't thought of for many years.

As Tom nears the end of this story it becomes clear that there is an intriguing connection between Claire and Emma. But is it real, or just a figment of imagination, brought on by a series of bizarre coincidences?